GREAT MOVIE
MISTAKES VOL. 2

Jon Sandys

THANKS

Thanks to ????, AAL117, Aidan2011, AidanN, Blickenstaff, Bruce Trestrail, Casual Person, Charles Austin Miller, David Mercier, Demmedelusive, Dr Wilson, GalahadFairlight, Garlonuss, Giacomo Chizzola, Grant Kneble, Grumpy Scot, Hamster, Hans Deutsch, ItsGav, Jack Kaltenbach, Jacob La Cour, Jason Hoffman, Jayson, Joe Campbell, Jon Sandys, Kit Sullivan, Krista, LadyArcher, LizzieWD, Low Cow, Lummie, Mark Bernhard, Mark Poliner, Matdan97, Matt Lynch, Michael Brown b6a7, Mister Ed, Mortug, Necrothesp, NoDouty, Oliver Hunter, P3ngu1n, PEDAUNT, Padzter, Pappy444, Phaneron, Quantom X, RJR99SS, Sacha, Scott215, Sean4000, Sereenie, ShooterMcGavin34, SoCalRuss, Spencer Crouse, Ssiscool, StephHugs, Steven moffat, Stonewall, Super Grover, T Poston, THGhost, TedStixon, Thumpback, Tonycdrive, Victor Meldrew, amycamille1975, demodon, eirik, flynn, furious1116, gandolfs dad, jbrbbt, keiko, kh1616, logan crews, manthabeat, mdwalker, mld172, paolog, poehitman, princesskelli, sam norton, shenry255, skeffderry, tedd, throcko, tokke, vejay25, virtual-toast, wizard_of_gore, zehner87, and all the anonymous submitters who helped make this book, and moviemistakes.com, what they are.

Thank you for buying this book! I hope you enjoy it, and if so please tell your friends, share it, lend it...spread the word! I'd love to hear any suggestions, corrections, thoughts and opinions - please get in touch at jon@moviemistakes.com. And please leave a review on Amazon - if you like this, there's plenty more where this came from. And if you've got any observations of your own, please submit them to moviemistakes.com and let other people know about them!

1

CONTENTS

Eraser (1996)

The Fast and the Furious (2001)

Frozen (2013)

Ghost (1990)

The Goonies (1985)

Grandma's Boy (2006)

The Green Hornet (2011)

Halloween (1978)

Harry Potter and the Deathly Hallows: Part 1 (2010)

Harry Potter and the Goblet of Fire (2005)

Hollow Man (2000)

Home Alone 2: Lost in New York (1992)

In the Bedroom (2001)

Jeepers Creepers (2001)

Jurassic Park (1993)

The Lord of the Rings: The Fellowship of the Ring (2001)

The Matrix Reloaded (2003)

The Matrix (1999)

Maze Runner: The Scorch Trials (2015)

The Mighty Ducks (1992)

Ocean's Eleven (2001)

The Purge: Election Year (2016)

Red Dragon (2002)

Resident Evil: Afterlife (2010)

The Rocky Horror Picture Show (1975)

Scary Movie 2 (2001)

Star Wars: The Force Awakens (2015)

Tarzan's Greatest Adventure (1959)

Thor: Ragnarok (2017)

Toy Story (1995)

Transformers: Revenge of the Fallen (2009)

Twitches (2005)

War of the Worlds (2005)

Visible crew/equipment

Back to the Future (1985)

The Birds (1963)

Chasing Amy (1997)

The Chronicles of Narnia: The Lion, the Witch and the Wardrobe (2005)

A Cinderella Story (2004)

The Dark Knight (2008)

The Descent (2005)

Ever After (1998)

Ghost (1990)

Gladiator (2000)

The Goonies (1985)

Harry Potter and the Chamber of Secrets (2002)

Harry Potter and the Philosopher's Stone (2001)

Harry Potter and the Prisoner of Azkaban (2004)

Independence Day (1996)

Jumanji: Welcome to the Jungle (2017)

Jurassic Park (1993)

Labyrinth (1986)

The Lord of the Rings: The Return of the King (2003)

Minority Report (2002)

Monty Python and the Holy Grail (1975)

The Nutty Professor (1996)

The Pacifier (2005)

Pearl Harbor (2001)

Pirates of the Caribbean: The Curse of the Black Pearl (2003)

Road Trip (2000)

Scream (1996)

Spider-Man (2002)

Spider-Man 2 (2004)

Star Wars (1977)

Teen Wolf (1985)

Three Musketeers (1993)

Titanic (1997)

Transformers: Age of Extinction (2014)

Troy (2004)

Twilight (2008)

War of the Worlds (2005)

Factual errors

2012 (2009)

The A-Team (2010)

Air Force One (1997)

Amadeus (1984)

Anaconda (1997)

Armageddon (1998)

A Beautiful Mind (2001)

Becoming Jane (2007)

Bird on a Wire (1990)

Body Heat (1981)

The Book of Eli (2010)

Brick Mansions (2014)

Bruce Almighty (2003)

Captain Phillips (2013)

Catch Me If You Can (2002)

Con Air (1997)

Die Another Day (2002)

Die Hard 2 (1990)

Dunkirk (2017)

Enemy at the Gates (2001)

Fast & Furious 8 (2017)

Flight (2012)

Fury (2014)

The Great Escape (1963)

Hancock (2008)

Independence Day (1996)

Indiana Jones and the Kingdom of the Crystal Skull (2008)

It (2017)

Journey to the Center of the Earth (2008)

Kingsman: The Secret Service (2014)

The Martian (2015)

Mary Poppins Returns (2018)

Minority Report (2002)

The Mummy (2017)

Murder on the Orient Express (2017)

Mysterious Island (1961)

Ocean's Eight (2018)

The Outsiders (1983)

Pirates of the Caribbean: The Curse of the Black Pearl (2003)

The Post (2017)

Spider-Man 2 (2004)

Spider-Man: Homecoming (2017)

Straight Outta Compton (2015)

Stripes (1981)

The Time Machine (2002)

Timeline (2003)

Titanic (1997)

Trainwreck (2015)

Twister (1996)

Wall Street (1987)

Plot holes

102 Dalmatians (2000)

3,000 Miles to Graceland (2001)

About Time (2013)

The Adventures of Tintin: The Secret of the Unicorn (2011)

Aliens in the Attic (2009)

American Dreamz (2006)

Battlefield Earth (2000)

Bolt (2008)

Broadcast News (1987)

Capricorn One (1977)

Casper (1995)

Coming to America (1988)

The Core (2003)

The Day of the Jackal (1973)

Die Hard 2 (1990)

Fast & Furious 8 (2017)

A Fish Called Wanda (1988)

Flight of Fury (2007)

Flight of the Phoenix (2004)

The Fly (1986)

Friday the 13th Part V: A New Beginning (1985)

Guns of Navarone (1961)

Halloween (1978)

Harry Potter and the Deathly Hallows: Part 2 (2011)

Harry Potter and the Prisoner of Azkaban (2004)

Hocus Pocus (1993)

Hollow Man (2000)

How to Train Your Dragon (2010)

Indecent Proposal (1993)

Indiana Jones and the Kingdom of the Crystal Skull (2008)

Little Giants (1994)

The Lost World: Jurassic Park (1997)

Midnight Run (1988)

Ocean's Eight (2018)

Ocean's Eleven (2001)

The Outsiders (1983)

The People Under the Stairs (1991)

Saw (2004)

The Shawshank Redemption (1994)

Silent Hill: Revelation (2012)

Skyscraper (2018)

Snakes on a Plane (2006)

South Park: Bigger, Longer & Uncut (1999)

Speed (1994)

Spider-Man 2 (2004)

The Sting (1973)

Superman (1978)

Ted (2012)

Teen Wolf (1985)

The Thomas Crown Affair (1999)

The Time Machine (1960)

Transformers: Revenge of the Fallen (2009)

Twister (1996)

UHF (1989)

Untraceable (2008)

Venom (2018)

Where Eagles Dare (1968)

Wrong Turn 4 (2011)

Revealing mistakes

10,000 B.C. (2008)

American Beauty (1999)

Austin Powers: International Man of Mystery (1997)

Austin Powers: The Spy Who Shagged Me (1999)

Casino (1995)

Charlie's Angels (2000)

Curse of Chucky (2013)

Fast & Furious 8 (2017)

Frozen (2013)

Ghost Rider (2007)

Gladiator (2000)

The Goonies (1985)

Grease (1978)

Harry Potter and the Chamber of Secrets (2002)

Harry Potter and the Order of the Phoenix (2007)

Home Alone (1990)

Hondo (1953)

Jack Reacher: Never Go Back (2016)

Jurassic Park (1993)

Jurassic World (2015)

Just Visiting (2001)

Lethal Weapon (1987)

The Lord of the Rings: The Fellowship of the Ring (2001)

The Lord of the Rings: The Return of the King (2003)

The Lord of the Rings: The Two Towers (2002)

Marley & Me (2008)

The Mask (1994)

Matilda (1996)

The Matrix (1999)

North by Northwest (1959)

Pirates of the Caribbean: The Curse of the Black Pearl (2003)

Plan 9 From Outer Space (1959)

Planet of the Apes (1968)

Road To Perdition (2002)

The Rocky Horror Picture Show (1975)

Scary Movie 3 (2003)

Something's Gotta Give (2003)

Spider-Man (2002)

Star Wars (1977)

The Sum of All Fears (2002)

Superman (1978)

Terminator 2: Judgment Day (1991)

Total Recall (1990)

The Twilight Saga: Eclipse (2010)

Willow (1988)

XXX (2002)

Audio problems

2012 (2009)

American Pie (1999)

Apocalypse Now (1979)

Back to the Future Part II (1989)

Beauty and the Beast (1991)

Blade Runner (1982)

Charlie's Angels (2000)

Charlie's Angels: Full Throttle (2003)

The Chronicles of Narnia: The Lion, the Witch and the Wardrobe (2005)

Cliffhanger (1993)

Clueless (1995)

Commando (1985)

Dirty Dancing (1987)

Dr. No (1962)

Dragonslayer (1981)

Drop Dead Fred (1991)

Eegah (1962)

Fargo (1996)

Friday (1995)

Furious 7 (2015)

Ghost (1990)

Hairspray (1988)

Halloween: Resurrection (2002)

Harry Potter and the Goblet of Fire (2005)

Hearts in Atlantis (2001)

Hot Shots! (1991)

Joe Dirt (2001)

Lethal Weapon 2 (1989)

The Lion King (1994)

The Lizzie McGuire Movie (2003)

The Lost World: Jurassic Park (1997)

Misery (1990)

Miss Congeniality (2000)

Mrs. Doubtfire (1993)

Napoleon Dynamite (2004)

The Neverending Story (1984)

Repo! The Genetic Opera (2008)

Scary Movie 3 (2003)

Scream 2 (1997)

Showgirls (1995)

Shrek 2 (2004)

Source Code (2011)

Speed (1994)

Star Wars (1977)

Star Wars: Episode I - The Phantom Menace (1999)

Star Wars: Episode III - Revenge of the Sith (2005)

Star Wars: Episode V - The Empire Strikes Back (1980)

Stargate (1994)

Terminator 2: Judgment Day (1991)

Thunderball (1965)

Tremors (1990)

V for Vendetta (2005)

The Wedding Singer (1998)

West Side Story (1961)

Who Framed Roger Rabbit (1988)

The Wizard of Oz (1939)

Character mistakes

The Alamo (1960)

Alien (1979)

American Pie (1999)

The Amityville Horror (2005)

Austin Powers: International Man of Mystery (1997)

Big (1988)

The Blind Side (2009)

Cadet Kelly (2002)

Clockstoppers (2002)

The Dark Knight Rises (2012)

The Day of the Jackal (1973)

Disturbia (2007)

Flight (2012)

Flight of the Phoenix (2004)

Full Metal Jacket (1987)

Fury (2014)

Gladiator (2000)

Gone with the Wind (1939)

Grease (1978)

The Great Escape (1963)

Halloween II (1981)

High School Musical 2 (2007)

The Holiday (2006)

Ice Princess (2005)

Independence Day (1996)

Jason Goes to Hell: The Final Friday (1993)

John Wick: Chapter 2 (2017)

Knight & Day (2010)

London Has Fallen (2016)

Mile 22 (2018)

Moana (2016)

The Pink Panther 2 (2009)

Pitch Perfect (2012)

Rambo: First Blood Part II (1985)

Ray (2004)

Runaway Train (1985)

Save the Last Dance (2001)

Scream 2 (1997)

Sex and the City 2 (2010)

Sherlock Holmes (2009)

The Social Network (2010)

Space Jam (1996)

Speed (1994)

Spy Kids 3-D: Game Over (2003)

Star Trek (2009)

Star Trek II: The Wrath of Khan (1982)

Stuart Little 2 (2002)

Swimming with Sharks (1994)

The Terminator (1984)

Transcendence (2014)

Underworld (2003)

Urban Cowboy (1980)

Vertical Limit (2000)

Where Eagles Dare (1968)

Without a Clue (1988)

Witness (1985)

The X-Files Movie (1998)

Deliberate mistakes

Ace Ventura: Pet Detective (1994)

Alien (1979)

Batman Returns (1992)

Beauty and the Beast (1991)

Beneath the Planet of the Apes (1970)

Beverly Hills Cop III (1994)

The Big Lebowski (1998)

Category 7: The End of the World (2005)

The Chronicles of Narnia: The Lion, the Witch and the Wardrobe (2005)

Final Destination 3 (2006)

Finding Nemo (2003)

Get Smart (2008)

Gladiator (2000)

The Great Santini (1979)

Harry Potter and the Chamber of Secrets (2002)

Ice Age 4: Continental Drift (2012)

The Interpreter (2005)

Jeepers Creepers 2 (2003)

The Lego Movie (2014)

The Lion King (1994)

The Lord of the Rings: The Fellowship of the Ring (2001)

The Lord of the Rings: The Return of the King (2003)

The Lord of the Rings: The Two Towers (2002)

Lost Treasure (2003)

The Martian (2015)

The Matrix (1999)

Meet the Spartans (2008)

Miller's Crossing (1990)

Miss Congeniality 2: Armed and Fabulous (2005)

Monsters, Inc. (2001)

Mr. Deeds (2002)

On Her Majesty's Secret Service (1969)

P.S. I Love You (2007)

Pearl Harbor (2001)

Peter Pan (2003)

Pirates of the Caribbean: On Stranger Tides (2011)

Pirates of the Caribbean: The Curse of the Black Pearl (2003)

Platoon (1986)

Scooby-Doo (2002)

Spy Kids 3-D: Game Over (2003)

Star Trek: Generations (1994)

Star Wars (1977)

Superman Returns (2006)

Taxi 2 (2000)

Top Gun (1986)

Toy Story (1995)

Transformers (2007)

Troy (2004)

X-Men 2 (2003)

Other mistakes

101 Dalmatians (1996)

12 Rounds (2009)

Ballistic: Ecks vs. Sever (2002)

Bambi (1942)

Basic (2003)

The Boondock Saints (1999)

Braveheart (1995)

Bullitt (1968)

Charlie Wilson's War (2007)

Charlie's Angels (2000)

CHIPS (2017)

Clue (1985)

Clueless (1995)

The Color Purple (1985)

Die Another Day (2002)

Die Hard 2 (1990)

Django Unchained (2012)

Drive (2011)

Dude, Where's My Car? (2000)

Dunkirk (2017)

Fantastic Voyage (1966)

The Goonies (1985)

Halloween 2 (2009)

Halloween: Resurrection (2002)

Hannibal (2001)

Happily N'Ever After (2006)

Home Alone (1990)

Home Alone 2: Lost in New York (1992)

The Hunger Games (2012)

Independence Day (1996)

Kong: Skull Island (2017)

The Lord of the Rings: The Fellowship of the Ring (2001)

The Lord of the Rings: The Two Towers (2002)

Mask (1985)

Midway (1976)

Mommie Dearest (1981)

The Mummy Returns (2001)

Old School (2003)

Passport to Paris (1999)

Pirates of the Caribbean: The Curse of the Black Pearl (2003)

Rampage (2018)

Resident Evil: Afterlife (2010)

Rudolph, the Red-Nosed Reindeer (1964)

Saving Silverman (2001)

The Secret of my Success (1987)

Shane (1953)

Sixteen Candles (1984)

Sneakers (1992)

Son of the Mask (2005)

South Park: Bigger, Longer & Uncut (1999)

Spy Kids 3-D: Game Over (2003)

Star Wars (1977)

Star Wars: Episode II - Attack of the Clones (2002)

Star Wars: Episode III - Revenge of the Sith (2005)

Sweeney Todd (2007)

Thunderball (1965)

Toy Story (1995)

Vacation (2015)

The End

ABOUT THE SITE
AND THE AUTHOR

I cannot lie - I haven't spotted all of these myself. After all, I've only got one pair of eyes, and only one lifetime! They've been accumulated over the past 20 years from myself and thousands of other eagle-eyed film fans across the world, and all stored on my website, moviemistakes.com. But rather than forcing you to trawl through the 100,000+ entries on the site, I thought it was worth selecting the cream of the crop for a book like this.

Back in September 1996, I was 17 years old, a huge film fan, and fairly computer obsessed. I wanted to make a web page, but couldn't really think of what to do. I eventually took a few continuity mistakes and film facts, put them into a website along with an e-mail address, and that was about it. Over time, thanks to word of mouth and the occasional bit of press, it's built into the collection it is today.

We love movies, but we also love to hate them. Some people love spotting mistakes in films to take Hollywood down a peg or two, but most people just view them as fun things to spot in their favourite movies which they'd never noticed after many repeat viewings. My experience tells me that spotting movie blunders is one of the most infectious hobbies there is, and if you share your observations with your friends or family, they'll catch themselves doing it too (and maybe even cursing you a little). And perhaps the phenomenon is infectious with any film directors out there, established or wannabe - and production people as well - and perhaps they'll start paying better attention too.

This book is primarily designed to point you in the direction of all those little things in movies that you may not have noticed the first, or second, or even third time around. It is for entertainment and educational purposes only. It should not prevent you from going go on with your life as normal. I take no responsibility when you're next watching a film and catch yourself thinking 'I'm sure her sleeves were rolled up in the last shot....' But, if after reading it, you no longer can watch movies without picking them apart for the most minute mistakes, I'm afraid there's only one piece of advice I can give you...you'll always find a home with similarly afflicted people at moviemistakes.com.

A NOTE ABOUT TIMES

Lots of the entries here have times after them, when the mistake happens in the movie. Due to the nature of different versions of movies, and especially the difference between formats, the times might be approximate. For example NTSC (used in the US) and PAL (used in lots of other places) mean times can be off by 4% (to do with frame rates - I won't bore you with the technical side here, but google will help you out if you're keen!). So if you're trying to find something and the time doesn't seem right, go forwards/back a bit and you should find the relevant scene.

HOW ARE MISTAKES MADE?

Films are hugely complicated to make, and all sorts of things can slip through the gaps, such as continuity errors, special effects equipment being a bit too obvious, film crew being in shot when they shouldn't be, and factual or historical errors. Continuity mistakes are far and away the most prevalent. Films are rarely shot in order - even single scenes can be shot out of sequence. As such, objects which feature in scenes can be moved between takes, stains can change shape, and even hair styles can change. Of course there are continuity supervisors whose job it is to make sure that everything stays the same between takes, but everybody's human, and not everything will be caught. There are cases where they can't be avoided. A good example can be seen in Mission: Impossible 2, where the tyres on the motorbikes change in the final chase scene from road tyres to off-road. Given the non-stop nature of the chase, combined with a change of road surface, there really was no way around it. Editing also plays a vital role in mistake creation - if scenes are cut out of a final version showing, for example, a slight change of outfit, then continuity mistakes occur. Even if they're easily explained, they're still movie mistakes.

Crew and equipment being visible can't be so easily justified. Aside from the rare occasions where a camera just has to be in a certain place, it's normally a case of carelessness or accident. The gas canister visible in the back of a chariot in Gladiator is a good example of this. Clearly in this case they could only do one take of the crash, so when the covering fell off, whether it was noticed or not at the time, they could only press on regardless. Mistakes like this tend to be more entertaining, but are also rarer.

None of these mistakes are meant to criticise the films they're a part of. Like everything in life, we can love something despite, or even because of its flaws, and having a few mistakes doesn't diminish a film's quality. I've yet to come across a flawless film, and to be honest I'd be surprised if one existed. Some visitors to the site seem to think I'm trying to pull Hollywood to pieces, which just isn't the case - no-one's perfect!

CONTINUITY MISTAKES

Something changing from one shot to the next, such as costumes or things in the background.

10 Things I Hate About You (1999)

When Kat and Patrick are playing paintball right before they kiss you can see that they are barely covered in paint. When they do kiss and are on the ground, they are totally covered with it. (01:06:35)

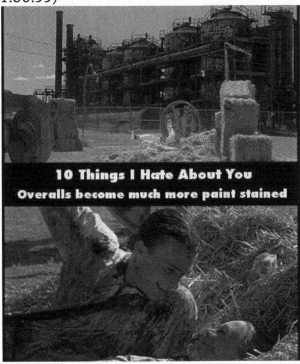

10 Things I Hate About You
Overalls become much more paint stained

Buena Vista Pictures

About Last Night (2014)

Towards the end when Debbie and Danny get into a fight around 5am at their apartment, Debbie packs some things and goes over to Joan's apartment to mull it over with her. While they're talking with Joan in her robe, Joan's hair goes from being up in a hairband (not even visible out of the hairband) to her hair being down and styled with no hairband at all and then back to up to not visible in the hairband again.

Aladdin (1992)

The tiger bites the seat off the suitor's trousers, allowing the viewer to see his polka-heart boxers. When we see the tiger in the courtyard, he has a part of the same boxer shorts in his mouth. So if he bit off the seat of the trousers, shouldn't he have purple cloth in his mouth? (00:11:45)

Aladdin
Trouser material becomes boxers material

Buena Vista Distribution Company

Alice in Wonderland (2010)

When Alice leaves to think over Hamish's proposal and chases after the White Rabbit, the heels on her shoes change, but when she falls into the hole the heels are back once again.

America's Sweethearts (2001)

When they are driving to the hotel both the limos have tinted glass, but when they arrive at the hotel John Cusack's limo no longer has tinted glass - we clearly see him inside the car, although the camera's outside.

American History X (1998)

When Danny gets shot at the end of the film, his paper flies out of his hand. But the very next shot of him shows that the paper is still in his hand being held over his head while he falls backwards. In one of the following shots the paper is back on the floor, but it's on the opposite side it should have been when it flew out of his hand. It's all shown in slow motion and it's very obvious.

New Line Cinema

Austin Powers: International Man of Mystery (1997)

When Austin and Vanessa are on top of the bus, for one shot Austin's teeth are clean.

Austin Powers: The Spy Who Shagged Me (1999)

In the scene when Mini Me and Young Number 2 grab for the cookies, when Young Number 2 grabs there are two, one that looks like chocolate chip, and a plain one. When Mini Me grabs for it there is just one. (00:52:35)

New Line Cinema

When Mini Me and Austin are fighting on the moon Mini Me bites Austin's spacesuit and you can see his British flag underwear. But after he sends Mini Me out into space, he drops the space suit and Austin is now wearing a blue jumper with no holes in it. (01:17:25 - 01:18:20)

Austin Powers: The Spy Who Shagged Me
Blue tracksuit appears under spacesuit

New Line Cinema

Back to the Future (1985)

When Biff and his goon friends are in Biff's car, as they chase Marty on his borrowed 'skateboard', the car's rearview mirror repeatedly disappears and reappears, and the side mirror changes from round to square repeatedly. (01:06:50)

The Beach (2000)

When Richard and Francoise are making love on the beach. They begin kissing deep under the water and continue all the way to the top. When they reach the surface they can stand up in the water which appears to be waist-level.

The Beach
From deep underwater to waist level water

20th Century Fox

Beauty and the Beast (1991)

In the 'Gaston' song sequence, near the end, Gaston is sitting in his huge antler chair with Lefou. In the wide shot, there is a bear rug behind the chair. The camera does a close up of Gaston, then in the next wide shot, the chair is on top of the bear rug. Also, after this, Gaston gets up off of the chair and in the next shot, both the chair and the rug disappear completely. (00:29:20)

Buena Vista

Belle opens the door outward so Gaston falls out, but after

she throws his shoes at him, she slams it shut from the inside. (00:18:00)

Blade (1998)

When Frost has the head pure-blood vampire on the beach, after he pulls out his first vampire tooth you see blood all over his mouth, but when it shows the closeup of him pulling out the other tooth, there is no blood. (01:04:22)

Blitz (2011)

When Brant kills Barry at the end of the movie, Brant lowers his gun after shooting him, but in the next shot he is pointing his gun at Barry. Also, the scene shows Brant holding a semi-automatic style handgun before shooting Barry, then when the scene pulls out it shows him holding a revolver, then shows him holding the semi-auto again.

The Bourne Identity (2002)

When Jason is cutting Marie's hair in the hotel room, his watch is on his left wrist. When he and Marie begin to kiss, in this flipped shot Jason's watch is on his right wrist, his moles have changed sides, and the hand-held showerhead behind them is backwards as well. Next shot his watch is back on his left wrist. The flipped shot has nothing to do with the small bathroom mirror. (01:00:56)

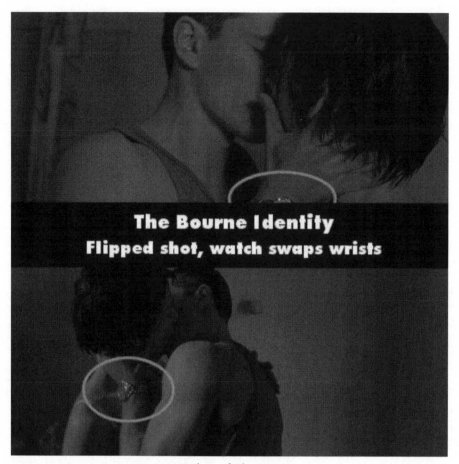

Universal Pictures

Charlie's Angels (2000)

Just after the explosion at the Angels' headquarters, Drew has soot all over her face, but in the final shot of her she's clean. Her hair's a lot neater too. (00:59:20)

Coyote Ugly (2000)

Violet drives through the toll booth on her way to sing her song. Then she says that she couldn't do it and made a big U turn. The toll booth wasn't that far behind her but it seemed like she drove a mile and a half before she reached it. (01:27:10)

Die Another Day (2002)

When Jinx and Bond sneak onto Grave's plane, Jinx can be seen with a nickel plated pistol (this is also evident throughout the entire film). Yet when Jinx is in the cockpit and Frost tells her to hand over the gun, it's now no longer nickel plated but standard gun metal black. (01:52:20)

MGM Pictures

When Bond first sees Jinx get out of the water, she is naturally dripping wet. After it cuts to him, it cuts back to her and she is already bone dry as she is picking up her towel to dry off. (00:34:55)

Dr. Dolittle 2 (2001)

When Dr. Dolittle is giving CPR to the bear, the bear is completely dry. If you just rescued something from the water, it should be wet. (00:35:30)

Driven (2001)

At the "Prototype Exhibition" party, Jimmy and Joe hop in two cars for a run through the Chicago streets. But, CART cars do not have built-in starters, they need external ones.

E.T. the Extra-Terrestrial (1982)

While Elliott and ET are saying goodbye, in the original 1982 version in the shot facing Elliott, ET lifts his right hand to point his finger at Elliott's forehead and ET's finger glows (note the weird angle of ET's raised right hand), but in the next shot facing ET when he says the iconic words, "I'll be right here," it's actually ET's left hand up by Elliott's face. This was digitally corrected in the 2002 version, so that in the first shot ET lifts up his left hand.

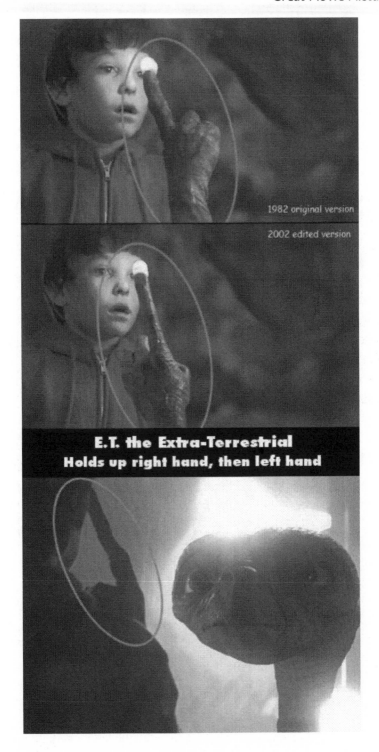

1982 original version

2002 edited version

E.T. the Extra-Terrestrial
Holds up right hand, then left hand

Universal Pictures

Eraser (1996)

Arnold goes to the gay bar to solicit the help of the guy he saved at the beginning of the movie. The guy is wearing a white shirt and a vest black/gold lamay. During their conversation he takes off the vest, then it cuts to another bartender. When it cuts back the guy has the vest on, another shot and the vest is off again. (00:08:05 - 01:10:50)

The Fast and the Furious (2001)

At the end of the movie, when Brian shoots the guy on the motorcycle, he gets out of the car and clearly shuts the door before crossing the street, but when he runs back to the car to chase Dom, the door is open. (01:34:23)

In the opening hijack scene, the semi obviously has two sets of rear wheels on the trailer, but when it comes to the scene where the black Honda is under the trailer, there is only one set of rear wheels. (00:01:11)

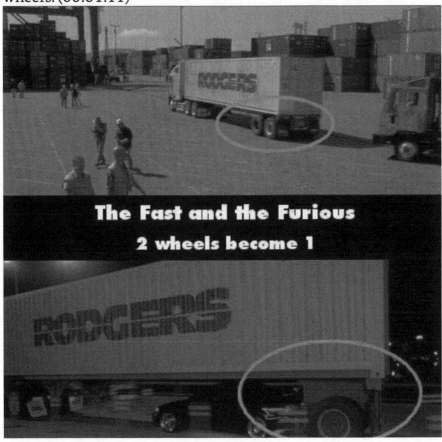

If you pay attention to the Supra at the end of the movie when he's chasing the dirtbikes, and when he's racing Dom you will notice that it switches from clean to very dirty many times. (01:29:53)

Universal Pictures

Frozen (2013)

When Anna, Kristoff and Olaf get thrown by Marshmallow, Anna does not have her hat on when they are sliding, yet her hat is back on in the next shot.

Ghost (1990)

Where Swazye and Moore are at the pottery wheel, seconds after their hands and arms had been smeared with clay, they're clean.

The Goonies (1985)

After the final correct bone keys are played, Andy is the last to cross, and in the close-up of her feet the map actually falls behind her into the hole, but it is back up in its proper place for Andy to make that last second grab for it. (01:22:25)

During the jail breakout, when Jake tries to open the ORV's door, in the shot facing Francis he is holding the gun in his left hand as he tries to open the door for his brother with his right hand. In the next shot facing Jake just before shouts, "I don't have the handle, open the lock!" Francis's gloved left hand is empty, and next shot, the gun can be seen in his right hand. (00:01:45)

Grandma's Boy (2006)

When they have rolled all the weed together, Dante lit the bong with both of his hands on the bong, but in the next shot he is just sitting back on the couch.

The Green Hornet (2011)

When Reid and Kato are fighting by the pool, the beach ball falls off the chair (beside the pool) when they land in the water, but is back up on the chair in a following shot.

Halloween (1978)

When Annie and Laurie leave the hardware store to go to their babysitting jobs it is broad daylight. When they reach the houses apparently just a few blocks away, it is already dark.

Harry Potter and the Deathly Hallows: Part 1 (2010)

When Xenophilius draws the Deathly Hallows symbol, he draws it so that the bottom of the line touches the bottom of the circle. The shot cuts away and back again when he draws the tri-

Jon Sandys

angle, but the line is no longer touching the bottom of the circle. (01:49:40)

Warner Bros. Pictures

Harry Potter and the Goblet of Fire (2005)

Straight after the second task Hermione wraps her own white towel round Harry, but between shots it jumps back to her shoulders, then back to Harry's several times. (01:35:05)

Harry Potter and the Goblet of Fire
White towel jumps back and forth repeatedly

Warner Bros. Pictures

Hollow Man (2000)

Why does the Twinkie Kevin Bacon eats disappear immediately? If things that go into him disappear, when they give the needle to the gorilla, you shouldn't see the needle point when it is stuck in her arm.

Home Alone 2: Lost in New York (1992)

In the first film, it is mentioned several times that Kevin is 8 years old. However, in this film it is stated that he is 10. When his parents are in the Miami airport security office, they say that he was left alone last Christmas. That would make him 9. Both films take place the same days, from about three days before Christmas until Christmas morning, so even if Kevin is born around Christmas time this is still a mistake.

In the Bedroom (2001)

In the kitchen scene, when Frank's parents are arguing, the clock reads about 6:45 and then in the next shot, it is 6:15.

Jeepers Creepers (2001)

About 10 minutes into the movie, when the truck is chasing the 2 college students in the car and starts ramming them, the bumper and the trunk is smashed in. The shot changes and shows the car's rear end and it is in perfect condition. This repeats at least 3 times.

Jurassic Park (1993)

When Tim and Lex first arrive, Lex is wearing a purple tank top with a colorful design, and in the following scenes or even between consecutive shots her tank top changes to completely different designs, though it's the same style of tank top.

Universal City Studios

The Lord of the Rings: The Fellowship of the Ring (2001)

As Boromir and Aragorn talk right before Boromir dies, you can see Boromir's right hand gripping Aragorn's left shoulder in the shot from behind Aragorn's right shoulder, but when the camera view changes to Boromir's perspective, looking up at Aragorn, his hand is not there. The scene goes back and forth between these two views several times. (01:22:40)

45

New Line Cinema

The Matrix Reloaded (2003)

During the freeway scenes, the katana Morpheus used as a foot hold to grab the keymaker keeps moving. It was at arm's length from the top when he inserted it; when Morpheus was standing on it, the sword was a whole body length below the top; when Morpheus took the sword out in his fight against the agent, it was back in its original position.

Warner Bros. Pictures

The Matrix (1999)

In the beginning of the movie when Neo gets the FedEx envelope, he is shown at his desk opening the envelope and then pouring it out. As he is pouring the phone out, with the green packing label on the top, the shot cuts "seamlessly" to a close up of the phone being poured out the rest of the way. However, the envelope is now flipped over. The FedEx logo is now on top (the packing label is facing down). (00:12:50)

When Neo is brought out of the building, you clearly see the police officer push the car door open and turn his head to the rear

47

of the car, yet in the next cut where we are viewing the scene from the reflection in Trinity's side view mirror his head is facing forward again. (00:16:00)

Maze Runner: The Scorch Trials (2015)

There are missing boys in the movie. At the end of The Maze Runner, there are 8 boys that get out of the maze besides Teresa. At the beginning of Scorch Trials, only 7 get in the compound. When Thomas shows the stolen card to the others, there are 6 of them and they all escape with Teresa and Aris. When they get out the mall and enter the city, there are 5 of them besides Aris and Teresa.

The Mighty Ducks (1992)

When Adam Banks is playing in one of the games, he scores a goal and his teammates on the bench stand up and cheer when he scores. Problem is, Adam Banks is on the bench too.

Ocean's Eleven (2001)

Linus and Rusty are standing in the Botanical Garden at the Bellagio going over Linus' observations. Rusty has a cocktail glass of shrimp in hand. When they change angles he has a plate in his hand, then change back, it's a glass. Full screen version. (00:43:40)

Ocean's Eleven

Glass turns into plate (then glass again)

Jon Sandys

Warner Bros. Pictures

The Purge: Election Year (2016)

When the Senator is about to be sacrificed, the cloth on her mouth immediately disappears for a split second. (01:29:35)

Red Dragon (2002)

When we first see Will Graham investigating the Jacobi household it is night time, yet once he is inside and heading up the stairs, the window behind him clearly shows daylight.

Resident Evil: Afterlife (2010)

Right after Bennett takes off in the plane, Claire throws a gun to Alice. Between the slow-motion shots, the gun switches position in mid-air before Alice catches it. In the shot of Claire throwing it, the barrel is facing to the right, meaning that it should be facing to the left in the shot of Alice catching it. But it still faces the right when she does. (00:58:30)

The Rocky Horror Picture Show (1975)

In the lab, during 'Hot Patootie', Eddie wears red suspenders clasped to his jeans. When he lies on top of Columbia, both back suspender clasps come undone, though the front clasps are still intact. In following shots both of Eddie's back clasps are on properly.

The Rocky Horror Picture Show
Red suspenders clasp themselves to pants

20th Century Fox

Scary Movie 2 (2001)

When Tori Spelling is lying in bed and the ghost pulls the sheet back and sees her ugly feet she doesn't have any socks on. As the ghost starts to have sex with her she has socks on. (00:30:30)

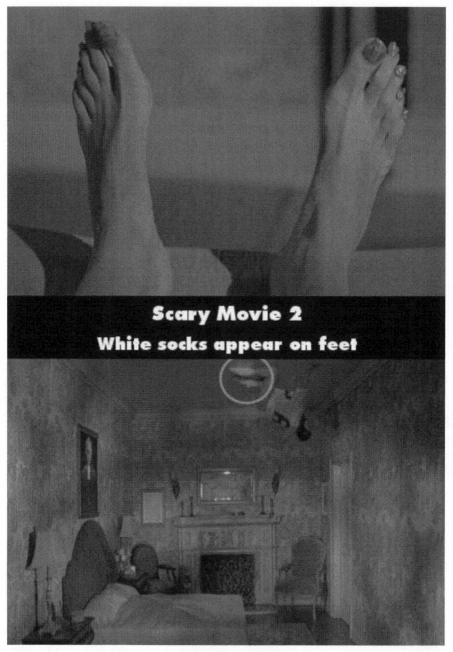

Dimension Films

Star Wars: The Force Awakens (2015)

After Rey touches Luke's lightsaber she begins to have the vision, and when she falls to the floor the blaster is missing from the back of her belt, but after she "sees" Luke and R2 and then stands up the blaster is back again, tucked into her belt. (Even though Rey's having her vision of things all around her, she herself is not a vision).

Star Wars: Episode VII - The Force Awakens
Blaster appears

Walt Disney Pictures

Tarzan's Greatest Adventure (1959)

In the scene towards the end of the film where we see Slade's body fall, it falls onto a submerged rock just below the surface of the water and there is a splash of water. In the next shot Tarzan looks down from the cliff above and Slade's body is on a large dry rock, a little distant from where the body originally fell.

Thor: Ragnarok (2017)

When Karl Urban is defending the Asgardians, the dust covers on his rifles vary between being open and closed several times. M16 dust covers are sprung loaded - they open on the first shot and have to be manually closed afterwards.

Toy Story (1995)

There's an electrical outlet on the wall below the window (aligned with the window shade's loop) in Sid's room near the Megadork poster, but when Sid throws Woody to the floor and raises the shade (before he scorches Woody's forehead with the magnifying glass), that outlet has vanished.

Toy Story
Electrical socket disappears

Buena Vista

Transformers: Revenge of the Fallen (2009)

After Mikaela throws the metal box at Alice and breaks the window, when Sam runs out of his dorm room screaming we see (and have seen multiple times prior to this) the wall and bathroom door opposite his door. Oddly enough, in the next shot from the hallway, Sam, Mikaela and Leo are actually leaving from a door that's farther down the hallway. Sam's actual door is the first one on the right, opposite the bathroom door - there is a bike wheel leaning against the wall beside the bathroom door. (00:52:00)

Twitches (2005)

During one scene in Camryn's Halloween birthday party (where she is wearing a silver mask), it is actually Tia playing this role instead of Tamera.

War of the Worlds (2005)

On the ferry, Rachel wears the purple/pink camouflage hoodie over her orange knit sweater with the colorful stripe sleeves, as usual. Now this is where things become strange. In the first shot as the trio come ashore, she is only wearing her orange sweater, she is not wearing the purple/pink hoodie - note the clear lack of fur hood. In the very next shot as they climb a bit more and then rest, Rachel is wearing the purple/pink hoodie - note the hood, but now it's on under her orange sweater. In the underwater shots she is also wearing it under the orange sweater. (This odd mistake has absolutely nothing to do with the very long wool cloak that Rachel wears in the next scene). (01:02:20 - 01:04:40)

VISIBLE CREW/ EQUIPMENT

Crew members, cameras, and other things that don't belong on screen.

Back to the Future (1985)

When the clock tower ledge breaks, Doc Brown slips and loses his grip on the electric cable. In the next shot the stunt wire pulling the thick electric cable towards Doc's pants is visible. (01:37:50)

The Birds (1963)

As Melanie drives up to have dinner at Mitch's the reflection of the cameraman on the inside of the window can be seen moving in the upper left hand portion of the screen. (00:32:10)

Chasing Amy (1997)

The cameraman is visible in the reflection of window while Holden is walking back to his car in the rain.

The Chronicles of Narnia: The Lion, the Witch and the Wardrobe (2005)

When Mrs. MacReady meets the Pevensie children at the train station, the reflector screen is reflected in the lenses of her glasses, as she looks down when she speaks to them. It is also visible when the children first arrive at the house, when Mrs. MacReady says, "There shall be no disturbing of the professor." (00:07:30)

A Cinderella Story (2004)

As Sam and Rhonda have Fiona's car confiscated, when Fiona runs out shouting, "I can pay for those parking tickets!" the crew's black mat is laid out on the walkway, but in the overhead shot when she tries to run away that mat is gone. (Visible on fullscreen DVD.) (01:28:10)

Warner Bros. Pictures

The Dark Knight (2008)

During Batman's interrogation of the Joker, when he picks him up and slams him against the wall, for a very brief moment you can see the camera and the cameraman in the reflection of the mirror on the right. (01:29:10)

The Descent (2005)

There is a shot of Holly crawling through a tight space with the camera facing her moving backwards and she crawls forwards (about 30 minutes into the film). In this shot, the wheel marks of the camera can be seen on the ground in front of her. (00:30:05)

Ever After (1998)

Near the end, when Rodmilla and her daughters are requested to appear before King Francis, in the first shot facing the king and queen, there is a beige narrow mat in front of the large patterned rug, which is not in previous or following shots, specifically used for crew/camera tracking. (01:50:30)

Jon Sandys

Ever After
Crew's beige mat visible

20th Century Fox

Ghost (1990)

When moving into their apartment Patrick Swazye kicks the statue to make it swing so they can get it inside. As they are looking at the statue, two moving men cross in back of them carring a mirror and as they pass you can see the director and camera crew in the reflection.

Ghost
Crewmembers visible in reflection

Paramount Pictures

Gladiator (2000)

When Maximus is told the Emperor is dead we see him barge past Commodus to see the body. Look behind Commodus at the roof and you should see an electrical stage light. (00:35:00)

During the scene where Maximus throws the sword into the crowd and yells "are you not entertained," the camera pans around, and in the crowd, for a split second, you can see a cameraman in jeans and a shirt standing next to a camera. This is visible on the big screen, but hard to see on video, unless you see it on DVD and can zoom in. (01:04:50)

During the first Gladiator match in Morocco, Maximus and Juba are chained together. Once they have killed the last man, the camera takes us around the arena. You can clearly see the shadow of the camera on Maximus' chest. It happens twice. (00:55:45)

When Maximus enters the arena before facing Tigris, the camera pans around the crowd. At one point, you can see a young Hispanic girl wearing a "scrunchie" holding her hair in a perfect ponytail, several bracelets and a watch, a necklace, a cut-off white t-shirt, and blue jeans. Most noticeable in full screen version. (01:42:40)

The Goonies (1985)

After doing the Truffle Shuffle, when Chunk walks into the Walsh's house, the reflection of crew/equipment is visible in the window to the right. (00:08:15)

Harry Potter and the Chamber of Secrets (2002)

Just arriving at Diagon Alley Hagrid says, "I was looking for Flesh-Eating Slug Repellent. They're ruining all the school cabbages." In the next shot Hermione exits the shop and runs towards Harry. On the ground is Dan Radcliffe's (Harry) red mark, which he promptly steps on just before Emma Watson (Hermoine) glances down and steps on her own black tape mark. (Visible on fullscreen DVD.) (00:17:20)

Harry Potter and the Chamber of Secrets
Actor's mark visible

Warner Bros. Pictures

Harry Potter and the Philosopher's Stone (2001)

In the scene where Hermione, Ron and Harry are returning to Gryffindor's tower room after being in the third floor room for the first time, you are able to see the feet of one of the crew. It happens just as they are passing through the picture hole, where Harry turns a couple of times to check that the "door" is closing. And it is in fact, because someone is walking behind it and pushing it shut, since the picture hangs several inches off the floor. (01:02:55)

Hermione opens the door to Fluffy's room when she says, "Alohomora!" so she, Harry and Ron could hide from Filch and Mrs. Norris. As Ron closes the door the top of the third floor corridor set is visible at the top of the screen. As an aside, when Ron repeats, "Alohomora!" look at Hermione's face. (01:02:00)

After the Queen attacks the Knight's horse during the chess

game, Ron goes flying back and falls. In the shot as he hits the ground, the black protective gear that he wears is visible when his grey T-shirt rolls up and the button on his left cuff is open, yet closed in the next close-up. (02:05:15)

During the Quidditch match as the players ride their broomsticks, visible in quite a few shots are the two wires that are attached to the broom handle, between their legs, that extend down with a clamped loop that goes around their feet. In some shots the wires between their legs are edited, but the wire loops around their feet are perfectly visible, like in the following example. When the Slytherin score hits 10 onscreen, in the next shot, as Flint shouts, "Take that side," the wire is completely visible at his right foot under his cloak. Two examples where the entire wires are visible are, when Flint grabs the club and says, "Gimme that!" the wires are blatantly visible and he then proceeds to slam the Bludger into Wood, who falls. Next close-up of one of the twins, the wires are visible before Flint starts to leap over him. (Don't confuse the cloak's long front ties for the wire). (01:19:00)

Harry Potter and the Philosopher's Stone
Foot loops visible

Warner Bros. Pictures

Petunia and Dudley enter the house when they return from the zoo, followed by Vernon and Harry. The crew's equipment is plainly visible on the ground beyond the doorway. Also, the pavement at the threshold extends far beyond the doorway and just before Vernon walks into the house, Vernon is visibly coming from the side of the doorway. In the earlier exterior shot when they stand by the car before they leave, as Vernon says, "I'm warning you now boy...," not only is the ground at the doorway completely different, there is a garden surrounded by white bricks beside the door, making it impossible for Vernon to have been standing there. (Visible on DVD fullscreen.) (00:05:40 - 00:08:05)

Harry Potter and the Philosopher's Stone
Crew's equipment visible beyond doorway

Warner Bros. Pictures

Dumbledore tells Harry that he will move the Mirror of Erised and not to go looking for it. In the following shot Harry walks outside in the snow with Hedwig on his arm. In the close-up of Hedwig, the jess (strap) around his left leg is visibly tethered to Harry's sleeve. The inside of Harry's sleeve also has a strap that secures the sleeve around Harry's wrist. Hedwig is obviously not tethered in the next shot. (01:36:45)

Harry Potter and the Prisoner of Azkaban (2004)

At dinner, just after Harry takes the plate from Petunia and as Aunt Marge says, "A bit more," referring to the brandy Vernon pours, in the left glass door of the hutch behind Vernon, there is a nice clear reflection of a crew member lowering his white sleeved arm off screen. (00:02:40)

Independence Day (1996)

When President Whitmore returns to the containment lab to see the live alien, just as Major Mitchell and a Secret Service Agent walk to face the smoke filled lab, the actor's mark is visible on the ground as the Agent steps up to it. (Only visible on fullscreen DVD.)

Independence Day
Actor's mark visible

20th Century Fox

In the containment lab, when the alien awakens and begins its attack, the alien moves from right to left towards a doctor, who is backed up against a door. The crewmember who is wearing the alien costume has on a white shirt and black trousers, and the costume's straps attached to the pants are visible, as well as some wiring at the back. (Only visible on fullscreen DVD.)

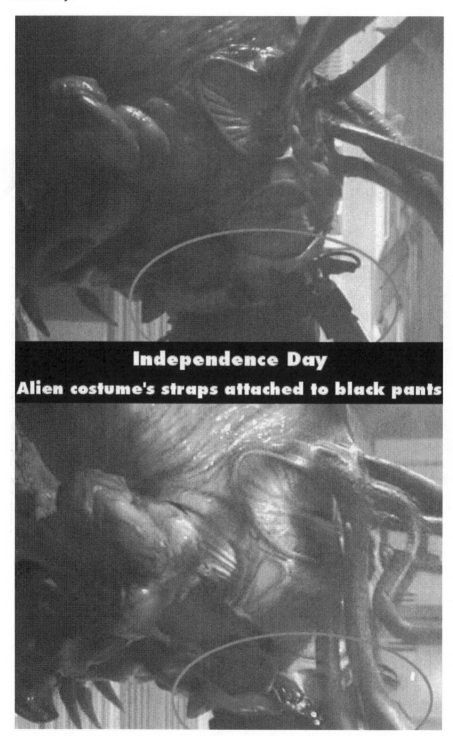

Independence Day
Alien costume's straps attached to black pants

After Dr. Okun unlocks "the vault" he explains the aliens' tele-pathic ability, and as David steps closer to the tanks the actors' marks are visible on the floor. (Only visible on fullscreen DVD.)

Independence Day
Actors' marks visible

Jumanji: Welcome to the Jungle (2017)

The scene where Spencer throws the boomerang for the first time and misses the bikers they take off running. While they are running from the bikers, there is a shot right before the boomer-ang hits the bikers where you can see a camera man sitting in the bushes on the left side. You don't have to pause it, but can to see it better. (00:36:30)

Jurassic Park (1993)

Watch carefully the scene where the raptors enter the kitchen (that angle where you can see almost the whole kitchen while raptors are coming in from the far away door). As the first raptor enters the kitchen, you can see someone grabbing its tail to hold the puppet-thing steady. (01:44:40)

Jurassic Park
Hand comes in to steady velociraptor

Universal City Studios

Labyrinth (1986)

Jareth says, "Sarah, don't defy me," and tosses the snake at her neck. In the next shot facing Sarah as she holds the snake, a crew member's hand is seen holding the end of the 'snake' below her right shoulder. (00:13:25)

After Sarah meets Sir Didymus at the Bog of Eternal Stench, Sir Didymus climbs on Ludo's back. While he is up there, the bottom portion of Didymus' right hand 'puppet control rod' is seen being controlled on Ludo's right side. The top portion of his right hand control rod is seen many times throughout his shots. His left hand control rod is concealed as his staff. (00:58:20)

When Sarah and Hoggle are in the Bog of Eternal Stench and they almost fall in, look in the top left hand corner of the overhead shot and you will clearly see a boom microphone. (00:53:40)

Sony Pictures Home Entertainment

In Goblin City, six guards gather together and one says, "Steady men. Hold your ground." The huge boulder comes rumbling towards them and hits them head on. In the wide shot as they lift off the ground, the tall pipes that create the white smoke are seen beneath them. (01:24:35)

The Lord of the Rings: The Return of the King (2003)

In Shelob's lair, when Frodo is caught in the web, in the first close-up while hanging there the camera pans down to his feet. Both ankles are wrapped and have foot supports and the wire cables attached to his ankle straps are visible, especially his left. In the next back shot, as Frodo turns around the wrist/arm support at his right arm, while he holds Sting, is seen too. (01:42:30)

New Line Cinema

When Sauron's forces start to surround Aragorn et al. at the Black Gate, there is a close-up of Éomer glancing towards the right of the screen. The next shot is of Orcs advancing to left of the screen. Fourth frame in, a dark haired crew member is visible behind the Orcs near the center, click some more and again he and others are visible in the background. (02:32:55)

Minority Report (2002)

When Anderton visits his wife after the auto plant scene, the camera pans around the car and the camera operator is clearly seen in the reflection on the bumper. (01:57:05)

Monty Python and the Holy Grail (1975)

In the scene where the knights are attacked by the killer rabbit outside the cave, you can see the boom mic at the top of the frame.

The Nutty Professor (1996)

At the party towards the end, Sherman leaves and Carla comes after him. As she runs toward him, the battery pack slides down her leg.

The Pacifier (2005)

When Shane is talking to Mrs. Plummer before she leaves, throughout the scene the camera man is reflected in her window (he is in black, not to get confused with Shane's white shirt) and as the car drives away the camera is shown backing up in the black door.

Pearl Harbor (2001)

After Evelyn tells Rafe that she is pregnant, she walks away and leaves him standing by the gas pumps. The camera zooms out and a boom mic comes into view in the upper right hand corner. (02:17:25)

Pearl Harbor
Boom mic dips into view

Touchstone

Pirates of the Caribbean: The Curse of the Black Pearl (2003)

At the blacksmith shop, Jack and Will start to duel and Jack asks, "But how's your footwork?" In the next close-up shot of their feet, the imprint of a modern, flat bottom trainer/sneaker sole can be seen on the dirt floor at the bottom right of the screen. It is not the imprint of a heel and sole of the time period. As a point of interest, on the video version of this film there are multiple imprints visible. (00:23:25)

Buena Vista Pictures

When the dock master tells Jack, "Hold up there you. It's a shilling...," seen in the background on the left of the screen is a thatched roof enclosure. An orange aluminum ladder is sitting under the thatch. Many of the crew's orange aluminum ladders of various heights can be seen on DVD 2. (00:10:10)

Buena Vista Pictures

When Jack and Barbossa duel in the cave, Barbossa hits Jack in the face. Barbossa yells, "Aaaah," and Jack takes off running with his arms waving wildly in the air. In this shot, as Jack waves his arms, at the bottom right corner of the screen, the wood scaffolding that was built for the cave set can be seen near the rocks in the water. The cave set scaffolding can be seen being built on Disc 2 of the DVD. (01:57:20)

Jack is in one of the boats with Norrington and his men, at Isla de Muerta. Norrington looks through the telescope, saying that he doesn't care for the situation and in the wide shot, when Jack says, "Not if you're the one doing the ambushing," in the water, to the right of the boat, a crew member's green flipper can be seen coming up out of the water. The divers kept the boats steady while filming. (01:43:05)

PotC: The Curse of the Black Pearl
Crew member's flipper visible in water

Buena Vista Pictures

After Will tells Jack that he can get him out of prison, he lifts a wooden bench to use for leverage and says, "And the proper application of strength..." In the next close-up of the bench as it's positioned at the cell bars, a crewmember's fingers are gripping one of the bars at the bottom right corner of the screen. (This is only visible on VHS.)

Just after Will cuts the lines from the Interceptor to the Dauntless, the Interceptor is shown leaving. The next shot is of the back wood plank between the ships falling away. On the deck of the Interceptor, behind the railing, on the right of the screen, is a crew member ducking down, so as not to be seen by the camera. (00:47:10)

Before being marooned on the 'spit of land,' Elizabeth stands on the Pearl's gangplank. In her close-ups, with the island in the distance, the long 'metal pipe' guardrails are visible behind her in three shots where she is still wearing the dress. The pipes are also visible behind Johnny Depp (Jack) in three shots, including when Barbossa says, "That be the same little island we made you governor of..." In all other shots of the gangplank there are NO guardrails surrounding the actual gangplank while it's extended over the water. (This is only visible on VHS, but can also be seen on DVD 2 and DVD 3 - 'The Lost Disc'.)

Buena Vista Pictures

Road Trip (2000)

In the scene when Josh and Tiffany go into her dorm room after the mail room scene; Josh goes to close the door and as he does a mysterious hand catches the door from the outside and closes it for him.

Dreamworks Distribution LLC

Scream (1996)

At the end when Sidney's dad falls out of the closet, if you look closely you can see the hands of a crewmember who was in there too, pushing items out after him.

Spider-Man (2002)

When Peter stands up after being bitten by the spider, there's the reflection of the cameraman with headphones on the television set behind him. (00:10:00)

Spider-Man 2 (2004)

On the way to the theater Peter intercepts a police officer chasing a couple of criminals. At the end of that scene one of the police cars has a tremendous wreck that swings the car sideways. There is a clear shot of the driver with a black helmet on.

Spider-Man 2
Police car driver wearing crash helmet

Star Wars (1977)

In the original widescreen version, during a long shot of a loading bay in the Death Star, you can see a crew member walk just into shot on one side of the screen, stop, look up, and back out again.

Teen Wolf (1985)

Michael J. Fox is dancing on top of a bus as the Teen Wolf. The camera swings just a little too far toward the back of the bus and a police car that is escorting the camera car and bus is seen in the rear with its red lights going.

Three Musketeers (1993)

In the fight scene on the stairs near the end of the movie, the camera shot looks up and there is a security camera mounted up in the corner. (01:29:40)

Titanic (1997)

When Jack comes to the first class door for the first time in his tux, you can see a cameraman in the glass door before he enters. (00:54:55)

Titanic
Camera reflected in door

Paramount Pictures

Transformers: Age of Extinction (2014)

Just after Lockdown stabs Optimus in the chest with his own sword, Cade runs closer and shoots at Lockdown. He then hides behind some bricks. In that shot, the bricks are a broken wall that is two separate pieces. Then it cuts to a different shot as Lockdown returns fire at Cade, and now the wall is one piece. Not only this, but some random guy suddenly appears in the shot next to the wall and right where the explosion happens where Lockdown shot the wall. He is wearing the same color clothes as the wall and only visible for a moment. There was no other guy present until that moment and he just suddenly appears behind Cade and gets hit. It's presumably a special effects member setting off the charge in the wall by the looks of it and it detonated before he got out of the shot. (02:30:55)

Paramount Pictures

Troy (2004)

As Achilles' ship nears the Trojan shores, Agamemnon snidely asks, "What's the fool doing? He's going to take the beach of Troy with fifty men?" At the start of the next shot, as the camera begins to pan down, on the far right, just beside a person's (who is dressed in blue) head is a metal bullhorn (ie. used to give instructions to cast/crew, and which definitely doesn't belong in this time period). (00:36:35)

As the 'Trojan' horse is being pulled into the city of Troy, in the cable-cam shot, just after the camera passes over the last of the riders on horseback, it passes a wood structure on the left, beside the large columns. Inside is a man in a black tee shirt, standing beside another man who holds an HT (handie-talkie - a two-way radio) up to his mouth with his right hand, as he points with his left hand. Then when the cable-cam spins around, they and a white tee shirt guy are visible down below. As a side note, there are some in the crowd that make eye contact with the camera and follow it as it passes (the cable-cam is not the POV of anyone - it sails over people's heads in the opposite direction than the 'Trojan' horse is being brought). Before it nears the wood structure, a woman on the ground below raises both her arms to wave and smile directly at the camera as it passes over. (02:17:10)

As the Trojans let loose their arrows on the Myrmidons, there is a close-up of a fiery arrow in a man's thigh. Two shots later, in a close-up of a Myrmidon stuntguy when he slams onto the sand, he clutches in his right hand a wired remote with a white trigger button, presumably to set off the little dramatic sand explosions as he lands. (00:39:50)

Jon Sandys

Warner Bros. Pictures

After Achilles, Odysseus and the rest exit the 'Trojan' horse, Odysseus signals the soldier at the top of the city's wall. When this soldier waves the torch in the wide shot, crane equipment leans over the interior wall, above the huge doors. It is obviously gone in the next wide shot of the wall, as the soldier continues to wave the torch. (Only visible on widescreen version.) (02:19:50)

Warner Bros. Pictures

84

Twilight (2008)

When Bella pulls up in her truck for her first day at Forks High, as the camera pans from her truck as she parks it into shot, you can see the camera and boom reflected in the triangular window. (00:05:35)

Summit Entertainment

War of the Worlds (2005)

In Mary Ann's kitchen, just as Ray comments, "Ok, well you hungry? I'll get you some food," the clear reflection of a male crewmember moving around is visible in the glass window behind Ray. Then just as he says, "This is ketchup and mustard," another older male crewmember is visible directly in front of Rachel's reflection. (00:35:45)

FACTUAL ERRORS

Historical/geographical mistakes, or other real world errors.

2012 (2009)

In the poster shot and in the film, the wave from the Atlantic carrying the carrier JFK into a collision with the White House comes crashing in from the west because the south portico of the White House is seen. The Atlantic Ocean is east of Washington, so the wave should come from the other direction. And even a wave coming from the east could not have made the JFK (CV-67) crash into the White House because the carrier was retired in 2005 and is berthed in Philadelphia, which is northeast of Washington DC.

The A-Team (2010)

They are present at Frankfurt, Germany. But with a closer look you see a cathedral at the right side. This cathedral and the central station are located in Cologne, Germany - they are about 220 km apart. (01:04:15)

Air Force One (1997)

The plastic explosive used on the cockpit door was C-4. When shot (as shown), C-4 does not explode; it requires the use of a detonator.

Amadeus (1984)

During the scene where Mozart is being carried away in his coffin by horse and cart there is a brief shot where he is being taken down a muddy path and a farmer is seen with his cows. If you look closely to the left side of the screen you can see a large overhead power line. If you look even more closely you can even see the wires coming out of the pylon. The movie is set in the 18th century and obviously it should not be there. (02:50:50)

Anaconda (1997)

During the first battle with an Anaconda, the 55-gallon fuel drums lashed to the deck of the riverboat are swept over the side, where they sink to the bottom of the river. This plot device drives the rest of the movie, since the boat must make a dangerous detour through "Anaconda country." There is just one small problem with this: Fuel drums full of diesel fuel or gasoline float on water. The fuel in them makes them buoyant. It would have been a simple matter for someone to get a rope or a boathook and retrieve the fuel drums before they floated away.

Armageddon (1998)

The surviving space shuttle takes off from the asteroid horizontally, like an airliner taking off from a runway. This is absurd. There is no air to provide lift for the wings, so the shuttle - with its engines providing thrust straight back - would simply trundle along the ground like a car. It doesn't use its maneuvering jets at any time, and they are far too feeble to lift the weight of the shuttle anyway. Nor do they gimbal the main engine, which would lift the shuttle vertically on an axis through the centre of the engine - they swoop gracefully into the air after a long take off. Second, they'd have to count on finding a clear length of ground on a debris strewn asteroid. Vertical takeoff, anyone?

Okay, we know the astronauts can walk around on the asteroid because they have those thrusters. So how is it, then, that the pilot can walk around the shuttle without anything to keep her on the ground? She should be bouncing around like the moon walkers.

A Beautiful Mind (2001)

The baby's pacifier that was used was not made at that time. It looked more like a NUK than the old rounded rubber tip.

When John Nash returns from the Pentagon to his place of employment, he walks by an American flag. The flag has the staggered row arrangement of the current 50 stars, not the 48 star flag as it would have been in the 1950s.

Becoming Jane (2007)

It's late 18th, possibly early 19th century and, as Jane and her sister walk along the beach, a construction crane is visible on the horizon.

Bird on a Wire (1990)

Mel and Goldie board a ferry. A visible sign states 'Detroit-Racine Ferry'. Detroit is on the east side of the state of Michigan but Racine, Wisconsin is west of Michigan, across Lake Michigan. The only water route to get from Detroit to Racine would be to circumnavigate the entire state of Michigan.

Body Heat (1981)

Regardless of how bad an attorney he is, Ned Racine must surely know that his acquittal for murder is a shoe-in. It's very doubtful that the prosecution would have even held out for remand in his case, and in fact they probably would not have even charged him in the first place. The fact that his fingerprints are on Edmund Walker's glasses is irrelevant. He and Racine were seen in public together, notably in the restaurant, and he freely admits to being in Walker's house. He could have handled Walker's glasses on any one of these occasions. The conversation Racine has with Ted about building the firebomb cannot be used in court, as Ted fires Racine as his lawyer at his second meeting; everything from the first is covered by attorney-client privilege. Maddy obviously isn't around to give evidence, and the yearbook entry Racine finds throws suspicion on her (and away from Racine) immediately. There are no witnesses and no forensic evidence, in fact there is nothing to support the prosecution case except a vague suspicion based upon his having had an affair with the widow-to-be. No court in the US would entertain the case for a minute.

The Book of Eli (2010)

The type of book that Eli is protecting would actually be just a fragment. The complete Bible, in braille, occupies as many as 18 volumes.

Brick Mansions (2014)

The "brick mansions" are in Detroit, but when the surveillance satellite footage is shown, the initial, close-up skyline shown from above is of San Francisco. Then as it zooms out it's looking at Chicago. (01:04:00)

Bruce Almighty (2003)

At the very end of the film Bruce is reporting on a drive for blood donors, and Grace leads him over to the booth to give blood himself - he is even wearing a tourniquet. However, he is supporting himself on a walking stick - he is not fully recovered from the injuries he received when he was run over, which happened when he was hit by a moving car - injuries which left him clinically dead. There is absolutely no way that a person who has suffered life threatening injuries and has undergone the (inevitably) intensive drug therapies and surgical procedures involved while under treatment in hospital in the fairly recent past would be allowed to give blood. There is no way that the Red Cross (or the US equivalent) would want to encourage people who have recently been hospitalised to try to give blood. Not only would that be the height of irresponsibility, they would be wasting precious resources and staff time turning away people who would not be allowed to give blood.

Captain Phillips (2013)

In the scene where the Navy Seals are riding in the cars, the VA state vehicle inspection can be read from behind. It read "6 13" for June 2013. This would have been correct for the period the film was made, but not for the time of the incident.

Catch Me If You Can (2002)

On the plane, while being escorted by FBI agents, Frank Jr sees New York's LaGuardia Airport and says, "There it is, LaGuardia Airport, runway 44." A runway numbered 44 is impossible. No runway can be numbered over 36 because there are 360 degrees in a circle. (01:58:25)

Con Air (1997)

The whole basis of the trial and conviction of Cameron Poe is a crock. The judge can not arbitrarily mete out a sentence that is harsher based on the ability of someone to defend him/herself. In justifying the harsher sentence because of Poe's military skills, the judge effectively says that Poe is more guilty than an average person due to his honorable and decorated service in uniform to his country. In my entire time in law school, I never read one out of the literally hundreds of cases I was assigned in which a judge issued a harsher sentence because of someone's innate or learned abilities to defend themselves. But since this was a movie court room proceeding, the fact that Poe had a witness to the fight (his wife), the fact that he was injured in the fight, and the fact that his uniform was torn and otherwise ruined as a result of the fight are never examined. A D.A. wouldn't have taken this to a grand jury on a bet, because they would have never returned an indictment or "true bill."

Die Another Day (2002)

During the scene in which Bond escapes from MI6 custody, after inducing drop in heartbeat, he seizes the defibrillator paddles and uses them to shock the two male orderlies. However, only one of those paddles would have administered a shock; the other one is only there to form a circuit for the electric charge, therefore, at best it should only have shocked one of the orderlies. (00:25:15)

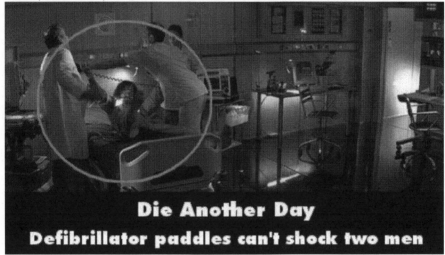

MGM Pictures

Die Hard 2 (1990)

When McClane is trapped in the cockpit of Esperanza's plane, and the terrorists throw grenades in, it sure takes them a *long* time to explode. At least a good 20 seconds passes before he ejects from the plane and the grenades go off. Normal grenades would have gone off long before 20 seconds.

The payphone McClane uses in Dulles airport has the "Pacific Bell" logo. Pacific Bell is a West Coast phone company. (00:04:20)

Die Hard 2
West Coast's Pacific Bell in Dulles Airport, VA

20th Century Fox

Dunkirk (2017)

In several scenes, but notably very near the end, the background shows numerous container handling cranes, which weren't invented until the mid sixties. (00:51:40)

There are a number of scenes of the buildings along the coast where TV antennae are visible.

Enemy at the Gates (2001)

When the map of the German advance is shown, Switzerland is shown to be taken over. Switzerland was never invaded by the Germans. (00:05:10)

Fast & Furious 8 (2017)

Throughout the "Manhattan" race scenes, it is obvious that the location is nowhere near New York. The wide two-way streets, west coast-style traffic signals, street furniture, and architecture look nothing like Manhattan.

Flight (2012)

Whenever the fire extinguisher is activated for a jet engine, that engine becomes inoperable. In the movie, the co-pilot first activates the extinguisher for the left engine, and 30 seconds later, for the right engine. At that point, both engines should be shut down. However, the engines are still operating (and revving up) and Whitaker even asks Margaret to apply full power, which is also audible. (00:23:00)

During the emergency, Whip instructs Ken to dump fuel, and fuel is seen spraying out of the nozzle on the wing. MD-80 family aircraft are not equipped with fuel dump capabilities.

Fury (2014)

During the final battle, Gordo the tank driver calls out, "Panzerfaust, four o'clock!", as he looks through his periscope. He could not have seen any targets at four o'clock, as the driver's periscope could barely rotate towards the eleven and one o'clock positions, close to the left and right front corners of the tank's hull. The four o'clock position would be near the right rear of the tank.

The Great Escape (1963)

Many of the prisoners are wearing watches, which is incorrect. Upon arrest a prisoner's watch was confiscated. This prevented them using them to bribe or barter with corrupt guards (and as this film acknowledges, there were plenty of those) as well as making coordination of meetings or escape plans difficult.

A convoy of open trucks arrive at the camp bringing the latest batch of prisoners, many of whom are carrying rucksacks and tote bags of clothing and other possessions. Where did they come from? Combat servicemen in World War Two did not carry overnight bags with them - a change of clothes or a handy supply of toiletries was the least of their concerns. A prisoner of war arrived in the camp with the clothes he stood up in and nothing else.

Why is Hilts not wearing a uniform? A serving officer captured behind enemy lines in civilian clothing risked being shot as a spy. If a prisoner's uniform was too worn or damaged to wear, it was routine for the German authorities to replace it - a P.O.W. in civilian clothes is an obvious escape risk. He is wearing a pair of tan chinos and a cut off sloppy Joe sweatshirt, both ridiculously anachronistic - Sixties hipster fashions - and nowhere even close to a World War 2 uniform.

Hancock (2008)

Basic physics - Hancock throws Michel from a dead stop to above cloud level in about eleven seconds. The clouds are bog standard cumulus which form at around 7,000 metres in temperate zones. This means that Michel accelerates to about 700 metres per second instantly, from a dead stop. Obviously he cannot accelerate during his ascent, so his starting speed has to be at least that. (In fact he would have to start his ascent much, much faster than 700 metres per second as he would be constantly decelerating due to gravity and air resistance, but it will do as a start point.) Michel accelerates from 0 to 2,520 kilometres per hour - twice the speed of sound - in zero seconds. He would be accelerating at around 5000 Gs, turning him into a very long streak of fine, pink mist.

Independence Day (1996)

During the final battle over Area 51, Russell Casse appears in his F-18 and states he is armed. After he attempts to acquire radar lock on the alien's primary weapon, he states he is locked on and has tone. He then says the tactical brevity code Fox-2, which indicates the launch of an infrared-guided missile. However, the missile he is actually attempting to launch is an AIM-54 Phoenix, which is an active radar guided missile, designated by the launch code Fox-3. The master monitor display also incorrectly shows the missile mounted on the port wingtip launcher of the aircraft where the AIM-9 Sidewinder would normally be mounted, instead of on the port wing's weapon pylon where the missile actually is. Historically, the F-14 Tomcat was the only fighter capable of carrying the AIM-54, as it was such a heavy missile; the AIM-54 was never used on the F/A-18. Instead, they carry the AIM-120 AMRAAMs, not the AIM-54 Phoenix that were shown in the film.

The Capitol's dome crumbles like stone, but it's made of iron. (00:48:10)

When Steven Hiller is flying through the canyon he says "Hope you got an air bag" and pulls a lever to deploy the braking chute on his FA-18. The chute is then detached and lands onto the attacking alien craft. FA-18's don't have a braking chute, they rely on using an arrestor hook for carrier landings and a dorsal airbrake when landing on a runway. (01:00:50)

When Jasmine is running in the tunnel, she kicks open the door just in time to save herself, her son, and the dog. The terrible fireball then goes right by them. They are just inside the open door, with fire and debris flying right past it. While the fire and debris might not spill in, the heatwave would still fry them. It is also likely that the fire would deplete the limited oxygen of the enclosed space. (00:49:50)

Indiana Jones and the Kingdom of the Crystal Skull (2008)

The 1950s kitchen scene shows a sink faucet "Dishmaster Model 87" which wasn't manufactured until 1987. The 1950's "Dishmasters" were different.

It (2017)

During the opening scene, a silver TV from the late 90's/early

00's is in the living room/dining room area. (00:02:10)

Journey to the Center of the Earth (2008)

Hannah's full name is Hannah Ásgeirsson. Icelandic surnames are (Father's name) sson for boys and (Mother's name) dottir for girls, so Ásgeirsson would be the surname of the male child of a man named Ásgeir. Her name should be Hannah Sigurbjörnsdóttir.

Kingsman: The Secret Service (2014)

When the barracks are completely flooded, Eggsy punches through a large two-way mirror to escape. The fact is that any glass (or plexiglas) thick enough to withstand many tons of water pressure without bursting would be as impenetrable as concrete to Eggsy's bare fist. He would need a chisel-tipped jackhammer to penetrate such a mirror.

The Martian (2015)

After Watney patches the blow out of one of the HAB's airlocks with plastic sheeting, tie down straps, and duct tape, he pressurizes the HAB and the plastic sheeting pushes out like an inflated balloon. Assuming the plastic and duct tape would hold this is correct, however the plastic would be much more taut given the pressure difference inside and outside. The real mistake is later in the scene during a sand storm the plastic flops in and out. The plastic would remain tautly inflated, since the inside pressure is much greater than outside, and since the HAB is airtight the storm would have no equalizing effect to cause the plastic to be sucked inward.

Mary Poppins Returns (2018)

Mr. Dawes Jr. states that the tuppence (two pence) invested by Michael grew into enough to pay off the mortgage on the house. Interest rates over that 20 year time period were about 4%, which would have made that 2p grow to all of 4p. Go nuts and assume an impossibly high return of 15% per annum, compound, consistent over the twenty years. Despite the fact that not even Bernie Madoff offered ridiculously high returns like that, after twenty years the original two pence investment would be worth 39p. As an aside, houses of the time cost about £750, far below current London prices, but still considerably more than 39p.

Minority Report (2002)

When Anderton jumps on the back of the jet packed cop, the thrust can sizzle burgers a foot away, but nothing happens to Anderton's jacket or shoes or anything. Even if he is hanging onto him on the side, he's still close enough. And how come the cops themselves don't get scorched by their own pack? I can believe them using asbestos pants in the uniform, but not Anderton's civvies. (00:47:55)

The Mummy (2017)

It is roughly 120-135 dB inside of a C-130, especially one that hasn't been specifically modified. It is so loud that it is painful to be in the cargo hold without hearing protection (besides it being outside of military regulations) and you certainly couldn't have a normal conversation while it was in flight.

Murder on the Orient Express (2017)

Before arriving at Brod station the train goes through high mountains. Between Belgrade (Serbia) and Brod (Bosnia and Croatia) it is all flat with no mountains around.

Mysterious Island (1961)

It is barely credible that a young Victorian woman like Elena would even think about wearing a goatskin miniskirt - exposing her legs in those days would be akin to walking about topless nowadays. Even if she did those bright yellow cotton knickers - gleefully visible in the scene in the beehive - are in no way from the 1860s. Her pants are a hundred years ahead of their time.

Ocean's Eight (2018)

Rhianna is watching a live feed of a man's office via webcam. We see a closeup of the screen. At the top it shows the filename being a ".jpeg." Jpegs are still image files, not movies, let alone live streams.

The Outsiders (1983)

The trains in this movie set in 1965 are from Burlington Northern and the St Louis and San Francisco Railway (Frisco). Burlington Northern was not around until 1970.

Pirates of the Caribbean: The Curse of the Black Pearl (2003)

During Jack's sliding down the rope scene, it is very noticeable that each one of the English soldiers fire their weapons more than once, which is impossible for that time, knowing that repetition weapons weren't invented until the mid 1800s. (00:20:00)

The Post (2017)

Robert McNamara is wearing a multi colored Polo shirt talking to Mrs. Graham in 1971. The Ralph Lauren Company did not make the shirts until 1972.

Spider-Man 2 (2004)

Considering the brightness of the fusion process, Dr. Octavius has to wear special goggles to be able to see it. Yet no one else in the room is wearing such goggles or seem hurt by watching the whole process, just as at the end of the movie. When welding something, no one can look at the arc that's created, as it would hurt his eyes and burn his retina; presumably, the fusion process would be brighter and more powerful than that, and so should have some kind of damaging effect on everyone's eyesight (except Spider Man's, maybe).

Spider-Man: Homecoming (2017)

The ferry splits in half down the middle, enough so the water is flooding in dramatically as the split grows. There is no possible way that the two halves of the ferry could have remained afloat like that. It would have sunk immediately. Then, as Iron Man "welds" the two halves back together, the ferry is afloat at the same waterline as before the incident, certainly not feasible with all the water it took on.

Straight Outta Compton (2015)

Eazy-E sports a black Chicago White Sox hat with a white logo early in the movie in 1986, but the logo didn't officially rollout until 1991.

Universal Pictures

Stripes (1981)

Then, as now, every recruit reporting to boot camp would be tested for illegal drugs, first by a urine test and then by a broad spectrum blood test in the case of a positive result. There is no reason for Elmo to try to hide his stash when the recruits are told they are to be tested - he is going to come up positive anyway. He may as well just say he has changed his mind and walk away. He is entitled to do that any time up to ten days after he signed on, and it happened a lot in real life!

The Time Machine (2002)

When Philby and Alexander are talking about Albert Einstein, Alexander mentions that Einstein is a patent clerk. The beginning of this movie takes place in the year 1899. Einstein was still in school and didn't become a patent clerk until 1902.

Timeline (2003)

When Lord Oliver states who he is at war with, he also asks about the Spanish. The Spanish at the time were not unified, instead he probably would have referred to them as the Castilians or the Aragonese.

Titanic (1997)

Rose mentions Austrian psychoanalyst Sigmund Freud's ideas on the male preoccupation with size to Bruce. However this is 1912, and Freud did not publish the work relating to this until 1920 in "Beyond The Pleasure Principle." Also, up until 1919, Freud relied solely on data from women. (00:33:40)

Trainwreck (2015)

When Amy is fired from S'Nuff magazine she takes her story on Aaron Connors to Vanity Fair, who run with it. That is not going to happen. Amy wrote the article while a paid employee of S'Nuff magazine and that means the copyright in the article (and, very relevant to this issue, the photographs of Aaron they paid to have taken), resides with them, not with her. It isn't hers to sell. No magazine editor of any standing is going to buy an unsolicited article without checking its provenance backwards and forwards, and that would mean checking with Amy's previous employers - after all, what would happen if they changed their minds and ran the story themselves?

Twister (1996)

In the begining when Jo's dad is bringing the family downstairs and say's "TV says it's big, might be an F-5" That scene was set in 1969. In reality he would not have known anything about an F-5 or any tornado with an F rating because the Fujita scale was not developed until 1971. (00:02:45)

Wall Street (1987)

The opening shot (of the New York Stock Exchange's trading floor) has the subtitle "1985," which might lead one to expect that at least the action in the first few scenes takes place in the year 1985. However, when Charlie Sheen is talking to his Nimrod broker buddy the Nimrod jokes that the day the Challenger exploded, Gekko was on the phone "selling NASA stock short." The Challenger exploded in January, 1986, not 1985. [An explanation for this: Wall Street, as conceived and filmed, was supposed to be set in 1987. However, near the end of 1986, The Ivan Boesky insider-trading scandal hit, many rules were changed, and acknowledging those events would have undone much of the plotting of the movie. So the movie was shifted back in time to 1985 (before the scandals, and also before the Challenger disaster), thus creating this major goof].

PLOT HOLES

Events or character decisions which only exist to benefit the plot, rather than making sense.

102 Dalmatians (2000)

When Fluffy saves Chloe she calls out 'thank you Fluffy'. Cruella never told her the dog's name so how did she know it?

3,000 Miles to Graceland (2001)

How could the police miss finding Cybil in the trunk of Michael Zane's car when it was in an impound lot? They would have definitely searched the car if he was found in violation of a federal offence (for carrying the weapons). Even if they didn't do a search, they would certainly have heard the sounds that Cybil would have made from being locked in the trunk.

About Time (2013)

They aren't able to travel before the birth of their children or their children become different. Despite that, he visits his father one last time before their third child is born. His Dad and he then travel back to when he was a kid, which would have changed his first 2 kids.

The Adventures of Tintin: The Secret of the Unicorn (2011)

In Bagghar, Allan knocks out Haddock by hitting him on the head from behind. Later, Haddock tells Tintin it was Allan who knocked him out - how would he have seen him?

Aliens in the Attic (2009)

In the scene where Ricky is fighting granny, she elbows Ricky in the neck and knocks off the alien control sensor. But later when he goes to the other girl's house, he is once again controlled by the alien joypad (without a sensor on his neck). (01:02:15 - 01:19:40)

American Dreamz (2006)

Cutting plastic explosive and disguising it as chewing gum will not hide the smell from bomb sniffing dogs.

Battlefield Earth (2000)

The barbarians find a working 1000 year old flight simulator. Beside the fact that the machine should not be working to begin with after such time, they were lucky enough to find a working power source in the barren wasteland.

Bolt (2008)

At the start of the movie, a great deal is made of the boom mic that enters the shot. This is ridiculous, because Bolt's view would not be restricted to what was onscreen, he'd have a perfect view of the person holding the boom mic (as evidenced by it not being stable). There's no possibility of him not seeing the person holding the mic either. As Bolt completely and utterly believes the world he lives in, and thinks the situations he finds himself in (saving Penny) are real, someone holding a boom mic would break the illusion for him. In all instances in the movie where an outside force (i.e. Dog handler) interacts with him, Bolt never gets to see the person handling him (handler approaches from behind), the boom mic operator however is literally right in front of him.

Broadcast News (1987)

How could Jane not be aware that Tom had only used one camera for the date rape interview, recording his fake tears later? That's the way things are done on television news shows and as an experienced, hard-bitten television producer she could not possibly be unaware of that. The reporter always records his or her reaction shots (called 'noddies') after the interviewee has left. Shooting with two cameras would involve two crews, two lighting rigs, a vision switcher and so on and so on and a straightforward interview simply would not justify such a complex and expensive set up.

Capricorn One (1977)

The "death" of the three astronauts and the requirement to then fake the whole scenario of the failed mission was obviously unplanned - it came about because of an unexpected computer glitch which reported that they had burned up on reentry, causing a mad scramble to cover up the fake mission and kill the astronauts. Obviously it was planned to have the astronauts "return" to Earth as heroes after their supposed trip to Mars, maintaining their deception (under threat if necessary) for the rest of their lives. One problem. Every scientist on earth would be champing at the bit to get their hands on a sample of Martian rock. Samples would be worth billions, worth far more than Moon rocks are worth today. How was NASA going to explain they didn't have any? They could not possibly fake the rocks - Martian soil and rocks would have a number of identifiable characteristics that a smart first year college student could identify. NASA have painted themselves into a corner and that is not something they would have failed to realise well in advance.

Casper (1995)

When Carrigan becomes a ghost, if Casper and no one else, including Dr. Harvey, can remember who they were; how does she all of a sudden know everything that has happened that is going on?

Coming to America (1988)

In the scene when Lisa and Akim are walking up to Akim's door (when Semi is sitting in the hot tub after fixing up their room), they are carrying groceries for Akim to cook Lisa dinner, however when Akim walks into the room (and every shot from inside the room) there is no kitchen for him to cook.

The Core (2003)

When the crew's vessel gets stuck in the giant geode and the crystal jams the 'impeller', the magma begins to fill the chamber. They see it melting the crystals, yet they frantically continue working to free the crystal from the impeller and lose a crewman...and yet when they get back in the vessel, the magma indeed melts out the crystal that jammed the impeller. With 2 geologists onboard you would think they'd know that.

The Day of the Jackal (1973)

An important plot point (in the book and the film) is that Charles Calthrop - thought to be the Jackal, at that stage - played some mysterious part in the 1961 assassination of Rafael Trujillo, the dictator of The Dominican Republic, and rumours of his involvement came to the attention of MI6 and Special Branch, leading to the accidental exposure of the Jackal's false passport. In fact there is no mystery at all about the assassination of Trujillo and there were no shadowy foreigners involved. It was organised by Trujillo's own senior aides, amongst them General Juan Tomás Díaz, Antonio de la Maza, Amado Garcia Guerroro and General Antonio Imbert Barrera. The gunmen was later identified as Luis Aniama Tio. All the conspirators except Tio were arrested, tortured and shot. There was no panicked evacuation of foreigners who were involved with Trujillo's regime and no reason for them to be concerned - the government did not fall and Trujillo's brother Hector took over as President, ruling in a brutal and totalitarian manner for a further eight years. Any rumours of a mysterious Englishman would have been dismissed out of hand and would not have made it onto even the lowest level filing system anywhere in Whitehall.

Die Hard 2 (1990)

The only reason the terrorists' plot can work is that the airports around Dulles are all closed to landings because of the violent snowstorm. If there were no storm, the pilots of the airliners in the holding pattern would simply divert to nearby airports when they started running low on fuel. If they were able to do that, the whole plot would simply fall apart. How were the terrorists able to count on the storm happening on the very day General Esperanza's flight was due to land? They didn't have any influence over the date of his flight. How did they know the storm would be so bad that all airports would be closed - except Dulles? I don't think they had any way of predicting the weather quite that accurately, and If the storm hadn't hit or had been even slightly less severe the pilots of the stranded airliners could easily have diverted to any one of half a dozen alternate landing sites, including a nearby Air Force base. They could do this without consulting or even contacting air traffic control. The whole plot falls apart from there - no hostages, no leverage, and who cares what happens to the people on Esperanza's plane? They'd have it shot down as soon as they knew Esperanza had killed the pilot and taken over the flight.

Fast & Furious 8 (2017)

The nuclear codes are stolen and the Russian guy holding them was let go by Dom. He would contact his government to let them know and the codes changed. Cypher would also know this so her plan is flawed.

A Fish Called Wanda (1988)

Shortly after the robbery, Kevin Kline and Jamie Lee Curtis get together in a little flat and Kline calls the police from a landline to tell them who committed the robbery. In England this would immediately lead the police to the flat from which the call was made, and the person reporting the robbery would be the first person the police would want to find and speak to. Otto has handed it to them on a plate. (00:12:29)

Flight of Fury (2007)

The admiral receives the news of the stolen aircraft from the general over an open radio, with umpteen enlisted personnel within earshot. However, when the air group commander asks what the OP is about, the admiral tells him that it is on a need-to-know basis.

Flight of the Phoenix (2004)

This film is set in 2004. The thought that no search and rescue operations would be put in place after an aircraft disappeared from radar during a routine flight is absurd. The Chinese are paranoid about intrusion on their territory and the downed aircraft would have been located by a simple satellite search within hours of it crashing. Chinese military satellites criss-cross the Gobi and they are equipped with optical cameras, microwave and infrared detectors and radar, so spotting a metal aircraft on the ground would be simple even if it was hundreds of kilometres off course. The crew would have been visited by Chinese military helicopters (and probably arrested!) as soon as the storm had died down.

The Fly (1986)

The whole problem with the teleporter occurs when fly DNA is mixed in with Seth Brundle's DNA, starting his transformation into the Brundlefly. Brundle is on a hiding to nothing from the word go, and the fly is irrelevant. Humans are a walking talking mass of foreign DNA - we are host to one trillion bacteria all of which has a complete compliment of DNA, as do various tiny mites that live in our hair follicles and all sorts of single cell organisms in our gut. If the transporter serves to mix the DNA of all living creatures which are in the transporter pod at the time Brundle would turn into a half-man, half-bacteria. Incidentally, DNA from a bacteria, an amoeba or a hair follicle mite would be just as 'compatible' with human DNA as that from an insect. It's quite a simple chemical, really.

Friday the 13th Part V: A New Beginning (1985)

When the cop shows Pam the newspaper clippings they include what look to be fresh photos of the real Jason from the events of Part IV, yet no photographer is ever seen taking pictures of Jason alive in the previous films and most likely wouldn't live long enough to publish the photo. (01:25:00)

Guns of Navarone (1961)

Maria describes in lurid detail how Anna was arrested by the Germans and tortured by being severely whipped, leaving her with gruesome scars all over her back. She also says that Anna hasn't spoken a word to anyone since she escaped from captivity. How, then, does Maria (or anyone else) know about the scars? Nobody saw them (they don't exist) and Anna obviously didn't tell anyone about them.

Halloween (1978)

We see Michael wearing the mask throughout the day, from morning at the Myers House, to mid-day outside Laurie's school, to afternoon when Tommy is leaving school, yet when Laurie and Annie see the sheriff in front of the hardware store on the way to their babysitting jobs (presumably in late afternoon or early evening), the store's alarm is still ringing and the sheriff mentions that one of the items stolen was a Halloween mask.

Harry Potter and the Deathly Hallows: Part 2 (2011)

One of Snape's memories show Lily telling baby Harry to be safe, be strong. That had to have occurred before Voldemort killed Lily. Snape was not in the house until after Lily was killed and Voldemort was gone. Only Lily and Harry should have had that memory, but not Snape.

Immediately after the confrontation between Harry/McGonagall and Snape in the Great Hall, Harry runs up to Ravenclaw tower against crowds of students running the opposite direction. However, all the students would have been in the Great Hall during that confrontation, and therefore would have been coming from the same direction as Harry.

Harry Potter and the Prisoner of Azkaban (2004)

Harry never notices that the name "Peter Pettigrew" appears on the Marauder's Map, right next to "Ronald Weasley." Way beyond a character mistake, as there's no way that wouldn't be cause for interest. If nothing else, Ron's brothers who had the map for years before giving it to Harry, would most certainly have wondered why their brother was sleeping with a person named Peter Pettigrew.

Hocus Pocus (1993)

After Max and Allison rescue Dani from the witches, Max is driving his parents' car. Winifred flies up along side of them and asks Max to show her his driver's permit. How would she know about driving permits, since she's been dead for 300 years?

Hollow Man (2000)

Where does Sebastian come from in the end when he grabs Elizabeth Shue? We would have seen him if he was on top of the elevator and he surely could not have been hiding in the fire.

How to Train Your Dragon (2010)

When Astrid gets on Toothless for the first time, Toothless takes off uncontrollably and tries to scare her. Hiccup seems to have no control over him at this time. How is that so if with the new tail fin, Toothless cannot fly without Hiccup's precise control of the tail fin? That whole sequence would have fallen apart. This mistake was even admitted to on the DVD commentary. (00:53:35)

Indecent Proposal (1993)

At the end of the film Woody shows what a nice chap he is by spending the 'tainted' million dollars at a charity auction. He's just made his problems much worse - he paid his solicitor a large fee to arrange the deal, so he hasn't got a million in the bank. That cheque is going to bounce so fast it will crack the plaster on the roof of the bank, and bouncing a million dollar cheque is a serious criminal offence in the US. (There is no way enough interest could have built up to cover the difference, either).

Indiana Jones and the Kingdom of the Crystal Skull (2008)

Hiding in a fridge (or anything else) in order to be conveniently blown out of the way by an exploding nuclear device is absurd beyond belief. The fridge is just so much extra reaction mass and will be vaporised by the expanding nuclear explosion - it will not be daintily picked up and thrown a few kilometers to safety. If it was, why doesn't it land in a shower of similar artifacts which have also been dislodged and thrown around? Incidentally, even if it was thrown out of the way as shown, anyone inside it would be turned into a smear of strawberry jam by the acceleration required to beat the shock and heat wave of a nuclear blast, and then liquefied by the deceleration involved in hitting the ground at that speed.

Little Giants (1994)

In the Cowboys' last possession of the final game, Spike makes a long run before being stopped on the goal line. The Cowboys' next play is a run up the middle. The Little Giants stop the run and the Cowboys lose possession, but since that was the first possession of a new set of downs, the Cowboys would have three more chances to score.

The Lost World: Jurassic Park (1997)

How did the men on the ship get killed? The bridge was intact and the T-Rex was still inside the cargo hold. [A raptor was meant to escape from the boat when it pulled into the harbour, but they cut the scene from the film and now that bit doesn't appear to make any sense.] (01:40:55)

Midnight Run (1988)

At the end of the film Mardukas reveals that he has been wearing a body belt packed with cash - "in the neighbourhood of three hundred thousand dollars" - ever since Jack detained him in New York. Are we to assume that Jack Walsh, an experienced, hard-bitten ex-police officer, now a bounty hunter who routinely chases down violent and armed bail absconders who would kill him without a second thought, didn't even perform a perfunctory search of Mardukas when he detained him? This man used to work for the Mafia! What if he was carrying a weapon? A body belt with three hundred one thousand dollar bills in it would be uncovered by even the most casual pat down.

Ocean's Eight (2018)

When Sarah Paulsen pulls the necklace out of the water, the necklace clasp is obviously closed. Since the circumference of the necklace is too small to fit over the top of Anne Hathaway's head, why would anyone believe that it fell off her when she

Jon Sandys

was running to the bathroom? The only way that could have happened is if the clasp (which we were earlier told can only be opened by a magnet) had opened. The trained security guards wouldn't have suspected something wasn't right about a closed necklace falling off over of her? They were following her. They saw that at no point did she lower her head on her way to the bathroom for the necklace to fall off over her head to begin with. It also could not have fallen off her when she was vomiting into the toilet in the bathroom since the clasp was closed. (01:18:25)

Ocean's Eleven (2001)

When Bruiser (the man who's supposed to beat up Danny) is faking the noises of punching Danny, the two thugs can hear him through the door. But earlier, he punched Danny by accident, then started to talk to him. The thugs should have been able to hear their talking through the door as well. (01:15:30)

The Outsiders (1983)

The pictures used in the newspaper article regarding the fire are obviously taken after Ponyboy and Johnny ran away since Pony's hair is blond and Johnny's is short (their hair was cut and dyed after they ran, ruling out the photos being old school photos), yet Johnny's face is free of burns. This would mean the pictures were taken while they were hiding in the church, which would be impossible.

The People Under the Stairs (1991)

The Man goes completely trigger happy shooting all the walls all around his house, trying to kill Fool, Leroy, and Roach at different points. The police come in and don't notice anything wrong. What about the bullet holes all over the place? (00:41:35)

Saw (2004)

Det. Kerry says at the scene of Paul's trap, "He had two hours." There is no way she could have known that. The clock simply said 3:00 and the tape specifically says "you have until 3 o'clock or this room will become your tomb". No way to know that's two hours after the fact. (00:17:30)

The Shawshank Redemption (1994)

When the warden comes into the cell the morning after the escape, the poster covering the hole is fastened down on all four corners - impossible to do after squeezing into that small hole. [On the DVD commentary, the director confirms that this was a movie "cheat".] (01:49:05)

Silent Hill: Revelation (2012)

The motivation of the cult in this film - a dark entity trying to birth their demonic god - is completely different from the cult of the original film, which was portrayed as fanatical Christian witch-burners. No satisfactory explanation is given in the film to explain this and in fact the film explicitly implies they are the same cult on several occasions. The explanation that the cult of the original film is some sort of offshoot or different sect of the cult from this film cannot explain this as it is pure fan speculation and conjecture (thus non-canonical) and in fact raises several more plot-holes.

Skyscraper (2018)

The entire plot hinges on the villain's gang obtaining the tablet that allows admin access to the building's systems. However, it can only be unlocked via facial recognition and it is keyed only to Will Sawyer's face. In fact, when they finally do get it, Xia unlocks it by holding it up to Sawyer's face. So what was the point of trying to steal the backpack containing the tablet? Without Will to unlock it, the tablet is useless.

Snakes on a Plane (2006)

The snakes are contained in the cargo hold which is shown to be unpressurised on this aircraft (there is an altimeter which releases the snakes after it hits 35000 feet - if the hold was pressurised it would level off at cabin pressure, which is about 8,000 feet). A cargo door is left open to allow the snakes into the passenger compartment, but this would either cause the plane to not pressurise properly, causing everyone on board severe breathing problems if not worse, or would keep the hold at cabin pressure, meaning the altimeter would never reach the right level to release the snakes.

South Park: Bigger, Longer & Uncut (1999)

The kids dig a hole and a spotlight goes over it. Wouldn't the operator notice the hole in the ground? (00:56:30)

Speed (1994)

If Jack can speed the train up, why does he not try to slow it down? Even if it can't be stopped completely, using the speed lever to reduce it to the minimum possible would be a sensible course of action. There is nothing to suggest he wouldn't be able to do this as he is able to increase the speed without any trouble. If there was something to show that slowing down the train would be unworkable it would make sense, but seems to more serve as a plot device.

Spider-Man 2 (2004)

At the end, when Peter saves Mary Jane from the collapsing structure, he jumps up in the air and swings her to safety. However if you look at the web he is holding onto it is hanging down vertically. What did he attach the web to that was directly above him, the sky? Every bit of the structure around him was/had collapsed and the only thing remotely close to swing from was the cranes. Yet we see that was quite a distance away, so

Peter would have had to shoot the web away from himself not above him. (01:47:50)

Spider-Man 2
Web isn't swinging from anything

Sony Pictures

The Sting (1973)

A vital plot line, obviously, is that Doyle wants to kill the con men who fleeced his runner of the numbers money. He has Luther killed and turns his best men (and women) onto Johnny Hooker, almost killing him, too. What about the third conman, Kid Erie? He is an essential part of the con, as much a part of it as Luther and Hooker. During the setup - just before they fleece him - the numbers runner watches Kid Erie running away. He looks at him, Hooker and Luther in turn. Even if he couldn't identify him he would still be able to inform Doyle that there were three rather than two con men involved. Even so, Kid Erie

comes and goes as he pleases. Doyle doesn't have anyone looking for him; he doesn't even mention him in conversation, and
in fact consistently refers to two - not three - con men. He makes
it clear that he would have to kill his best friend if he even found
out about the con, yet he lets one of the central participants go
scot free. It doesn't make any sense at all.

Superman (1978)

After Superman has reversed time the Hoover Dam reverts to its
previous undamaged state as it should, but Jimmy Olsen should
then have been replaced back on the dam. Instead he interrupts
the potential kiss between Lois and Superman and complains of
being abandoned by Superman in the desert.

Ted (2012)

Ted calls on John to tell him that he saw Lori leaving her apartment with her boss. How did he find him? He turns up not only
at the right hotel but the right room! They have had no contact since their fight after the party and Ted hasn't been asking
around after John as he tells him he 'just saw' Lori leaving with
her boss. So how did he find John? Is he psychic?

Teen Wolf (1985)

Isn't it rather strange that nobody outside the Howard family's
small town expresses any interest in the confirmed discovery of
a new human sub-species, the only one on the planet? Wouldn't
it be more likely that their little backwater town would be in-
undated with every press and scientific organisation on earth,
and that the Howard family would be the centre of the greatest
publicity carnival of all time?

The Thomas Crown Affair (1999)

When Renee Russo was reviewing the tape showing the room
with the painting to see who stole the painting, and the tape
was blank because the heat generated from the suitcase hidden

under the bench, why didn't she just back up the tape completely to see who put the suitcase there in the first place? (00:28:30)

The Time Machine (1960)

When George stops the machine for the first time, the candle burned down to about half of its size, which took according to his observations 98 minutes. But as the trip continues it takes seven hours for it to burn down completely. (00:25:45)

Transformers: Revenge of the Fallen (2009)

Simmons stands outside the 'The Monastery' at Petra (not to be confused with 'The Al Kazneh' at Petra where *Indiana Jones and the Last Crusade* was filmed) and looks at the horizon, and he is able to see the Air Force landing with Optimus by the pyramids. It then appears to take them mere minutes to drive over there. This is outright laughable, even accepting that they make the trip in an alien robot car. Petra and Cairo are separated by hundreds of miles of desert, not to mention Israel being between Egypt and Jordan.

Twister (1996)

Throughout the entire movie, barns, houses, cars, 18-wheelers, etc. are demolished and lifted into the air like they were made of paper. And yet Jo and Bill pass through one tornado after another with nothing more than their hair getting messed up a little. You'd think the debris alone flying into their faces at 100 miles an hour would be enough to give them a few injuries.

UHF (1989)

R.J. Fletcher is shown as a ruthless businessman who knows everything there is to know about Channel 62 - who owns it, how much it's worth, who is running it, the financial troubles it is having and so on and so on. He is also fully aware of the telethon and the fact that George is selling the station as a going concern for a total of $75,000.00. It is simply asking too much of audience credulity or 'suspension of belief' to think that such a hard-headed businessman would not work out that he could, using stooges, buy a controlling interest in the station for $37,501.00, saving himself a small fortune and closing the station down over the objections of his minority shareholders. Something this blatant could not possibly be a character mistake - he is already planning on buying the station for the full price (from Big Louis) so don't tell me he wouldn't just switch plans and buy it from George instead!

Throughout the telethon we see volunteers taking pledges over the telephone. As with all telethons the vast majority of pledges will be paid by cheque. Instant bank transfers were unknown in the days the film was set and the telethon ends at midnight, at which time American banks are most certainly shut! How does George manage to have $75,000 in CASH for Big Louie on site that very night? Not every single pledge would (or could) go out to the remote site to pay in cash - not at that time of the night, anyway - and he couldn't raise more than the required sum as this was a share offer and an oversell would reduce the value of individual shareholder's equity.

Untraceable (2008)

The FBI in the movie has the ability to "blackhole" an IP address, which makes that computer unavailable to the internet. If they can blackhole the computer acting as the *web* server, they could also blackhole the computer acting as the *name* server (DNS), thereby taking down the web site and preventing additional users from connecting.

Venom (2018)

At the angle of descent and the speed it was traveling (still burning from reentry even), when the space shuttle crashed in the opening of the film, it would not have left much of anything behind. The kinetic explosion that would have resulted would have downed the forest around it for a good distance leaving a crater, and the clean up crews would have been lucky to find any piece of the ship itself still intact bigger than a football. Much less been able to find any discernible remains of the crew. Yet bodies were being taken out in still relatively good condition. And probably most unbelievable is that the glass containers holding the Symbiotes were not even broken.

Where Eagles Dare (1968)

Why do all the Germans abandon the cable car control room after the alarm has been sounded? If the cable car is critical for access to the castle then you would expect a hard core of SS troops to remain behind to control access and protect the machinery in the event of an attack. (01:42:55)

Wrong Turn 4 (2011)

No one wonders what happened to all the staff and patients at that sanatorium? No police ever came there and checked the place out after 30 years? And all the patient records, furniture, etc are still there?

REVEALING MISTAKES

Anything which gives away filming techniques, such as stunt wires being visible, or glass smashing before anyone goes through it.

10,000 B.C. (2008)

After Evolet got hit by the arrow and presumably dies, D'leh is staring at a mammoth. Behind the mammoth, you can see that the background is a picture.

American Beauty (1999)

In the scene when Ricky's father rushes to his room and punches him, Ricky is bleeding before he is hit. (01:08:00)

Austin Powers: International Man of Mystery (1997)

In the scene at Alotta Fagina's penthouse, you can clearly see the side of her swimming costume as she gets in the jacuzzi - she's meant to be naked. (00:44:00)

Austin Powers
Swimming costume visible despite nudity

New Line Home Entertainment

Austin Powers: The Spy Who Shagged Me (1999)

In the scene where Mini Me is drawing the goodbye card to Scott, (before they go to the moon) you can see that the drawing is already on the page and Mini Me just traces it over. (01:05:50)

Casino (1995)

At the beginning of the film where Robert De Niro gets into his car and it explodes, you can clearly see the cut where they have replaced him with a dummy. (00:00:50)

Casino
Robert DeNiro replaced by dummy

Universal Pictures

Charlie's Angels (2000)

The caravan is shot-up with machine guns - so why are the bullet holes (the metal of the caravan's walls) bending outwards? (00:50:45)

When Drew is shot through the window, supposedly naked under the towel, you can see underwear when the shot is from below looking up, before she falls. As she falls down the hill, look closely and you can see the skin-tone suit she wears.

(00:57:50)

Curse of Chucky (2013)

When Nica crawls to the elevator to escape Chucky, she bends her legs in order to shut the elevator door. She is meant to be a paraplegic and have no feeling in her legs.

Fast & Furious 8 (2017)

On the ice the tank is firing - in slow motion we see empty shells are littering the area. The shells have crimped ends, revealing them to be blanks.

Frozen (2013)

After visiting the merchant, Kristoff's guitar has four strings, but only three tuning pegs.

Ghost Rider (2007)

In the day following the Rider's first ride, Cage shows up at the street that has been burned down the center. A person very close to the beginning of that scene walks on the broken up rocks and it moves as if it were a pad or a sponge. It wasn't a rock moving because the street moves with the rock. It happens a couple of times during that scene.

Gladiator (2000)

After the final fight scene, where Maximus is dead and on his back in the sand, his armour would have made his head droop horribly backwards. To avoid that, the filming crew put a pillow of sand under his head to raise it about three inches. (02:20:10)

Gladiator
Pillow of sand under Russell Crowe's head

Dreamworks Distribution LLC

The Goonies (1985)

At the start, when Data is being pulled towards the chained orange drum, due to the angle of the close-up, we see that the soles of Data's Nikes are not actually touching the ground (since there is a rolling mechanism under his feet). Despite the fact that Data is quite inventive, we see in the next shot there's nothing attached to Data's Nikes. (00:03:55)

Grease (1978)

In the soda shop, the waitress turns off the lights with her elbow because her hands are full, but she misses the light switch by 6 inches. (00:55:10)

Harry Potter and the Chamber of Secrets (2002)

During the car flight (on the way to Hogwarts) Harry and Ron have gone out of control outside Hogwarts. During the scene when the car is approaching the whomping willow the car is massively out of proportion compared to when the car is in the tree. (00:25:25)

Mrs. Weasley might as well knit like a muggle because she's not making any progress with magical knitting. In the Weasley's home and we see the magic knitting, the needle shoves into the hole, but no thread loops around and it is not advancing. The amount that has already been knitted is magic indeed since all the motion shown in the film produces no results. (00:11:25)

In the many and lengthy dialogue scenes between Potter and Dumbledore, with countless facial close-ups, neither of them have glass in their spectacles. (02:19:40)

Harry and Ron's trunks are being thrown out of the car and in the shot just before Harry's close-up, Ron's trunk (the other trunk says HP) slams down on the grass. The top of this trunk has a large perfectly symmetrical hole in the center with four round marks around it, which was probably involved in the throwing somehow. In the wide shot as Hedwig is being tossed out, the trunks are clearly visible and there is no hole in either, nor is there a hole in Ron's trunk at any other time. (00:28:10)

Harry Potter and the Chamber of Secrets
Mysterious hole in Ron's trunk

Warner Bros. Pictures

When Harry is fighting the Basilisk on top of the skull in the Chamber of Secrets, you can see that there is a safety tip on the end of the sword. (02:12:55)

When Harry and Ron run at the wall to get to Platform 9 3/4 if you watch Hedwig's cage when they tumble over you can see a toy bird that is glued onto the perch. (00:22:50)

Warner Bros. Pictures

Harry Potter and the Order of the Phoenix (2007)

In the Forbidden Forest, HRH are introduced to Grawp. Just as the giant lifts Hermione off the ground, in the shot from behind her, Hermione's legs disappear below her calves; the digital lines are actually visible. Slow-mo is not necessary. (Only visible on fullscreen DVD.) (01:29:40)

Harry Potter and the Order of the Phoenix
Legs disappear and digital lines visible

Warner Bros. Pictures

Home Alone (1990)

As Kevin is flying off the front porch on the toboggan, you can see the small wheels mounted on the bottom of the sled to aid in its "jump". (00:25:30)

Hondo (1953)

In the final Indian chase at the conclusion of the film, when a covered wagon rolls over, one can see the rope that was used to ensure it tipped over.

Jack Reacher: Never Go Back (2016)

When the leading hitman jumps from the balcony you see him land on a rubber mat.

Jurassic Park (1993)

In the scenes where there's a video link to the docks shown on computer, there's a bar moving along the bottom of the screen, showing us that it's actually a video that's just playing on the computer. (00:52:05)

Jurassic Park
"Live" video is recorded

Universal City Studios

Jurassic World (2015)

Inside Jurassic World's main control room, Chris Pratt looks at a view screen depicting a paramilitary team tracking down the escaped I-Rex. In an homage to the film Aliens, the screen is complete with POV cam footage and heart rate monitors. Unfortunately, the FX team didn't catch the fact that all four people are shown having identical heart rates. Ridley Scott made the same mistake in Prometheus. (00:44:00)

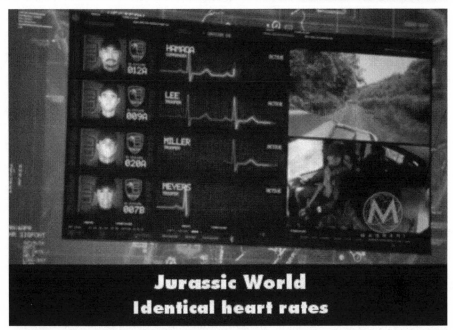

Jurassic World
Identical heart rates

Universal Pictures

Just Visiting (2001)

When the security guard finds the wizard as he appears on the bed, the guard's reflection can been seen in the doorway. (00:43:10)

Lethal Weapon (1987)

Riggs handcuffs himself to the depressed businessman. They jump off the building but they're not handcuffed to each other anymore. They used plastic cuffs which could separate during the stunt in case anything went wrong. They break just as they jump, so they grab each other's hands to stay in contact. After they land the cuffs are attached again. (00:31:00)

Jon Sandys

Warner Bros. Pictures

The Lord of the Rings: The Fellowship of the Ring (2001)

When Gandalf first visits Bilbo in Bag End they sit at a long table that is positioned lengthways from the camera. Bilbo potters about at the far end of the table and Gandalf goes to the left at the end closest to the camera. As he sits down the near half of the table wobbles but the far half does not. This seems to expose the fact that the table is actually in two parts, a small sized piece of table close to the camera next to which Gandalf looks large, and a normal sized piece of table a bit further away that looks the right size for Bilbo. The two pieces are filmed from such a perspective that they look like they join together in one long table and the fact that there is really a gap between them so that Bilbo is further away than it seems, makes him seem small compared to Gandalf. There is a round of cheese and various pieces of crockery on the near piece of table to disguise the gap. (00:17:10)

Once the secret door to Moria is open, when Gimli says, "Soon Master Elf, you will enjoy the fabled hospitality of the Dwarves," as Gandalf leads the way inside, note the glint of the trailing power cord as it moves along the ground behind Gandalf and goes directly under his robe. This is the staff's electrical supply cable. (00:16:20)

The Lord of the Rings: The Return of the King (2003)

After the Witch King destroys Gandalf's staff, the wizard and Pippin fall to the ground in the wideshot. In the next close-up, as Pippin (who is behind Gandalf) raises his right leg while he gets up, the white/black sneaker he wears is briefly visible on Billy Boyd's Hobbit foot. (Extended version). (00:24:10)

The Lord of the Rings: The Two Towers (2002)

When the women and children are evacuated to the Glittering Caves under/behind Helm's Deep, in the first shot, a hooded person leans on a stalactite making it sway back and forth. (00:51:55)

Frodo, Sam, Faramir and Gollum are at the sewer in Osgiliath when Faramir asks, "Cirith Ungol?" and then grabs Gollum's neck. Frodo and Sam watch as Gollum is grabbed, but their eyes do not follow Gollum as Faramir grabs him, their eyes remain focused on the ground to their left. The shot of Faramir and the shot of Frodo and Sam were edited together, with Gollum added later. (01:42:20)

Marley & Me (2008)

When John picks his wife up at the airport, it's raining. But look at the people around outside, they are in T-shirts, in the sun, and not getting wet. Obviously the rain is being sprayed on the car.

The Mask (1994)

When The Mask is dancing with Tina and he turns her into a human tornado while spinning her around, none of the on-lookers in the crowd show the slightest bit of amazement at the impossible feat that just occurred in front of them, indicating that the extras were not directed to react to the special effects.

Matilda (1996)

When Matilda telepathically makes the TV explode, you can see what looks like parts of an explosive hidden behind the screen.

The Matrix (1999)

When it is Neo's turn to make the Jump he takes a run up, and the camera changes to a brief sideshot of him running across the top of the building with the sky behind him. There is a big fuzzy blobby outline around him which should have been edited out. (00:52:20)

Warner Bros. Pictures

North by Northwest (1959)

In the shooting scene in the Mount Rushmore cafe, a boy in the background puts his fingers in his ears, because he knows the gun is about to be shot.

Turner Entertainment

Pirates of the Caribbean: The Curse of the Black Pearl (2003)

When the Black Pearl swings alongside the Interceptor for the battle, Elizabeth shouts, "Fire all!" The next shot is from behind the lit cannon which is aimed at the Pearl and the following shot faces the Interceptor's cannon, as it goes off. In the shot facing the Interceptor, the raw wood scaffolding type beams are perfectly visible at the entire lower part of the screen, where the painted planks (below the gun ports, above the bilges) of the hull should be. (This is only visible on the video version.)

PotC: The Curse of the Black Pearl
Set scaffolding in shot

Buena Vista Pictures

After Gillette locks the shackles on Jack's wrists, it is clear in Jack and Elizabeth's close-ups that the wider side of the shackles' distinctively shaped straight bar faces out at his wrists. However, when Jack is in the blacksmith shop, sitting at the anvil trying to break the links, the left shackle is actually around his wrist the opposite way. (This even occurs in other consecutive shots.) (00:19:00 - 00:21:30)

Plan 9 From Outer Space (1959)

When Bela Lugosi walks off screen, it's obviously a freeze frame. The swaying tree stops moving and even though he was hit by a car, his shadow is still visible. (00:07:55)

Planet of the Apes (1968)

Most of the posed, fake displays in the ape's Museum of Natural History contain real people who are slightly moving if one pays careful attention. Especially noticeable are those posing with objects held in - or above - their hands.

Road To Perdition (2002)

At the end when Sullivan is shot in the back while looking out the window, you can see blood come through the front of his shirt, meaning the bullets must have exited his body, yet the window he is standing in front of isn't shattered by the bullets that had passed through him. Also, immediately after this when Jude Law sets up his camera to take photos of Tom Hanks dying, the blood all over the glass is completely gone. The window is clean.

The Rocky Horror Picture Show (1975)

Funny how when Brad and Janet are led to separate rooms, their rooms are identical, right down to the folds in the chair material and missing drapery tassle fringes...

20th Century Fox

When Riff Raff and Magenta burst in after Frank's song, Janet steps away from Frank's side into Brad's arms. Watch Brad's face - you can clearly see the look of pain, as Janet steps on his foot in four inch spike heels. (01:24:55)

20th Century Fox

Just minutes after Rocky's creation, when he is lifted out of the tank, there is a nice close-up of Rocky's face. The newly created man with the "Charles Atlas seal of approval" has a few silver fillings in his upper right teeth, which are easily visible as he sings, "Over my head and I've got the feeling..."

Scary Movie 3 (2003)

A quick mistake happens when Brenda and the girl crawling out of the TV get in a fight. Brenda throws the punch, the other girl falls over, and for a quick second her dress flies up too far and you can see where the makeup (that makes her look dead) on her legs end and you can see her real thigh. (00:25:15)

Miramax Films

Something's Gotta Give (2003)

Right before Jack Nicholson sees Diane Keaton naked, there are shots of Keaton getting undressed. There is a close up of swollen feet that you can see are obviously not Diane Keaton's. The far shot shows her with smaller feet and legs.

Spider-Man (2002)

The scene at Columbia University was filmed on an unseasonably warm spring day, however, the costume department had provided the high school extras with cold-weather clothing. The real Columbia University students can be seen in the background wearing shorts and t-shirts by contrast. (00:05:35)

Star Wars (1977)

When the Tusken Raiders are seen raiding Luke's speeder, you can actually see the wheels or at least whatever is holding it up off the ground. (00:28:10)

20th Century Fox

On the Jawas' transporter, when R2D2 looks around in one of the shots, you can very clearly see the actor, Kenny Baker, inside through his eye hole.

The Sum of All Fears (2002)

In the scene where Jack Ryan uses the radio after the helicopter crash, the film is reversed - the word *frequency* appears as a mirror image.

Superman (1978)

Superman has fillings in his teeth.

Terminator 2: Judgment Day (1991)

When the Terminator's arm is caught in the wheel and he rips his own arm off and stands up, if you look closely (slow motion can help, but isn't essential) you can see his real arm stretched behind his back under his leather jacket. (02:09:30)

In the scene where the Terminator and the T-1000 are fighting in the corridors of The Galleria, the Terminator has fired multiple shots at the T-1000. When he gets up off the floor, the Terminator throws him into the left wall and the impact hole is already visible before he hits. (00:31:45)

When the Terminator is trying to save John from the T-1000 in the truck, he makes the jump. If you look at his face and hair while he's airborne, you can see it's a stunt double. The Terminator stunt double is also obvious in other shots throughout the film. (00:35:40)

Terminator 2: Judgment Day
Definitely not Arnie

TriStar Pictures

Total Recall (1990)

Doug has the hologram when inside the alien nuclear reactor, and a bunch of bad guys encircle the holographic image and fire at it at point blank with automatic weapons, and not one bad guy gets hit. If they encircled the 3D image, at least a few bad guys would have been hit by their own men. (01:37:00)

The Twilight Saga: Eclipse (2010)

After killing Victoria, Edward rips off a piece of Bella's shirt to tie around her bleeding arm. If you look at where he rips her shirt, the seam is visible where the fabric has already been cut and loosely reattached; there is a long horizontal wrinkle where it doesn't hang right from the rest of the shirt.

Willow (1988)

When they are at the Nutmar camp in the mountains, Val Kilmer tells Willow "Get on that shield!" but when they go over a 6, 7, 8 foot drop when they are sledding down the snow, you can clearly see runners on the shield.

XXX (2002)

The Senator's Corvette explodes before it hits the ground. (00:09:10)

AUDIO PROBLEMS

Anything related to sound, such as echoes in the wrong place, or speech not matching lip movements.

2012 (2009)

An early scene in the movie has Chinese soldiers recruiting Tibetans to work on a secret project which they are told is a dam. As the scene ends, the sound of explosives draws everyone's eyes towards the mountains, where the explosions can be seen several miles in the distance. The sight and sound of these explosions take place simultaneously. Sound travels much slower than light. In reality, there should have been some delay before the sound of the explosions was heard.

American Pie (1999)

In the prom scene just before Heather is looking around and looking bored, the drummer is tapping on the hi hat, but the sound is a crash cymbal.

Apocalypse Now (1979)

As Playmate of the Year Carrie Foster is brought out to the audience carried by two Green Berets watch the band behind her closely. The bass player stops playing as he scratches his head but the bass on the soundtrack keeps going. (01:07:55)

Back to the Future Part II (1989)

When Doc and Marty return to the year 1955, you hear the squealing sound of tyres braking heavily, but the DeLorean is flying. (01:02:25)

After Doc and Marty return to 1955 in an effort to steal the almanac back from Biff, they land the DeLorean. Doc says, "Here's some binoculars" then says "and" but watch his lips as he says "and", it just doesn't match. You could argue that it is a bad angle but even at the angle it's at, you get an OK view. (01:03:05)

Beauty and the Beast (1991)

When Mrs. Potts is talking to Belle for the first time, in her bedroom, Mrs. Potts says "It'll turn out alright in the end. You'll see." However, when she says "...you'll see" her mouth remains closed. (00:30:50)

Blade Runner (1982)

Deckard investigates the maker of artificial reptiles; an Abdul somebody. It's obvious that the dialogue was added as neither actor is in sync with the sound. The end of the scene has the storekeeper's voice telling Deckard the information he was seeking while Deckard's mouth is the one moving. Deckard's mouth continues to move even after Abdul's lines are finished and the scene cuts. This has been corrected in the 2007 Final Cut of the film, but exists in all previous versions. (00:48:45)

Charlie's Angels (2000)

In the sequence where Natalie is saving Bosley and calling Pete, listen carefully. When Bosley warns her that there are thugs behind her, he says Dylan instead of Natalie.

Charlie's Angels: Full Throttle (2003)

In the scene at the orphanage, when the boy runs down to the other boys reading the pornographic magazine, none of their mouths move when you hear "Look at those knockers".

The Chronicles of Narnia: The Lion, the Witch and the Wardrobe (2005)

When they're standing on the breaking ice, as Peter points his sword at Maugrim, Susan shouts, "Look, just because some man in a red coat hands you a sword doesn't make you a hero. Just drop it." In the very next shot (we still see Susan's profile, despite the side shot), Susan's lips/jaw are moving, but nothing is heard, which occurs just as Peter quickly glances at her and we also hear Beaver shout, "No, Peter!" (01:14:15)

Cliffhanger (1993)

After the two treasury agents restrain FBI Agent Mathison, Agent Travers draws his weapon and we hear the sound of him cocking the hammer, however, his thumb stays on the grips.

Clueless (1995)

When Cher and Tai are at the party and Travis comes up to them he has 2 cups of some kind of drink and all of a sudden you hear a sound that is supposed to be something spilling. I guess they assumed that it was supposed to be the beer spilling on Cher's shoes. Well as you can see nothing falls/spills from the cup, it is just sound effects.

Commando (1985)

The scene where Bennet and Matrix are fighting towards the end of the movie, before Matrix kills Bennet they have each others throat in their hands and one of their backs is against the furnace. While they are grunting and groaning, if you listen carefully, you can hear one of them say "switch" just before they change positions. (01:19:05)

When Matrix tells Cooke that "I eat Green Berets for breakfast" you never see his lips move when he says "right now I'm very hungry." (00:46:47)

Dirty Dancing (1987)

In the scene where Penny and Johnny are teaching Baby their dance routine you see Penny putting on a record, if you look closely you can see that Penny moves the arm to put the record on then right away you see her taking the arm away even though the music has started. Even if it's a directorial device for us to hear different music than they do, it's still a mistake because she's not actually put the record on, meaning they've not got any music playing. (00:36:35)

Dr. No (1962)

When Bond and Honey are on the beach the hoods of Dr No come by boat. On the boat there is a guy shouting through a megaphone. As they sail away again the man waves the megaphone to his comrades and says "full speed ahead". Yet his voice sounds identical to when he was speaking through the megaphone, though he isn't holding it to his mouth anymore. (01:04:00)

Dragonslayer (1981)

During the climax of the film, the maiden takes the stone from Galen and attempts to smash the amulet. Galen pulls the stone away and says "NO! He said I'd know the time". However, his lips do not match the words. He appears to say "NO! It is not yet time!"

Drop Dead Fred (1991)

As Fred slides down the banister he cries out "Whee!" but his mouth remains closed. (00:16:50)

Eegah (1962)

After Roxy, Tom, and Robert discover Eegah's footprint, Robert can be heard saying, "Watch out for snakes!" however his mouth does not move at all. (00:10:30)

Fargo (1996)

When Carl is being beat up by Shep, Shep is shouting a whole bunch of obscenities and gibberish at Carl, but during several shots where we see his face, the audio is not matched up to what he is shouting.

Friday (1995)

When Smokey is spanking the boy who knocks over the trash cans with his belt, notice he only spanks him a few times yet the sound of the spanks is double the actual amount.

Furious 7 (2015)

When Dom, Brian, and Mr. Nobody are in the car and Mr. Nobody says about trying the Belgian ale, he coughs and says another line. However his mouth doesn't move at all during this time. (01:26:00)

Ghost (1990)

At the end of the movie, Carl is chasing Molly and Oda Mae. He says something like "Molly she's a thief!" and something else, but his lips don't move.

Hairspray (1988)

When Corny introduces himself at the auto show, the audio is not in sync with his lips.

Halloween: Resurrection (2002)

When Myles is at the party in the office checking out the web broadcast, a guy and a girl bust in and intend to have sex there. What we hear the guy say doesn't match up with his mouth movements.

Harry Potter and the Goblet of Fire (2005)

In the scene right before the champions enter the maze, Cedric Diggory hugs his father, Amos. When they pull away, Amos says, "That's my boy," but his lips aren't moving.

Hearts in Atlantis (2001)

When Anthony Hopkins is talking to the boy, the boy is sitting in front of a mirror. Anthony starts talking to him, and the camera angle moves to behind Anthony. You can hear Anthony talking, but his lips aren't in sync to the reflection in the mirror.

Hot Shots! (1991)

Topper is driving in to the base beside the running troops on his bike. When they recite the Brady Bunch part, none of the soldiers' mouths are moving.

Joe Dirt (2001)

In the scene where the janitor is tap dancing in the hallway, the tapping sounds do not match up with the times that his feet hit the ground.

Lethal Weapon 2 (1989)

In the scene where Leo explains how he launders the drug money and Roger says "You're a cheat", Leo says "Come on, everyone cheats a little, look at the pentagon." But when he says "look at the pentagon", it's dubbed in because the sound of his voice doesn't match his other dialogue, and if you read his lips it doesn't match either.

The Lion King (1994)

(May only apply to the original VHS release.) When Scar has Zazu locked up in a cage, Zazu mentions Mufasa's name and Scar yells at him, "What did you say?" Right before Scar's actual line, whilst Zazu is talking, you hear Scar's "What did you say?" line very faintly in the background, even though Zazu has not even mentioned Mufasa yet.

The Lizzie McGuire Movie (2003)

When Lizzie is performing at the end of the movie at the awards show, at the part where we see her from the back facing the blue light, her voice sounds like it's changing. It seems like it's someone much older singing, or the synthesizer went wrong. It just obviously isn't Lizzie's voice anymore.

The Lost World: Jurassic Park (1997)

The ship is going at full speed towards the coast - making a roaring engine sound. But when it hits the coast and stops, the sound of the engines stop too. Who turned them off? (01:46:25)

Misery (1990)

In the scene where James Caan is lying in bed, practising grabbing a large knife from his arm sling, there is the metallic sound as he pulls out the knife. In the sling are his arm and the knife. There is nothing metal the knife could be pulled against to make that sound.

Miss Congeniality (2000)

When the final five contestants are being interviewed and Gracie does her 'if anyone hurts one of my new friends' speech, you can see that she says, "I will take them down," but it has been dubbed over so she says, "I will take them out." (01:31:32)

Mrs. Doubtfire (1993)

During the final court case scene at the end of the film, Miranda's lawyer turns to her and says, 'Congratulations'. The lawyer's head is turned away from our view slightly, but you can see that she doesn't move her mouth. It does move about a second after 'Congratulations' is said, but it does not move long enough for the lawyer to have actually said 'Congratulations'.

Napoleon Dynamite (2004)

When Napoleon knocks on Trisha's door he knocks four times but you only hear three knocks. (00:38:05)

The Neverending Story (1984)

When Nighthob and Teeny are talking to the Rockbiter near the beginning of the film, Teeny says to Nighthob "This could be serious", then turns to Rockbiter and calls out his name. Watch Teeny's mouth as he calls out "Rockbiter". You will see a very blatant editing mistake as Teeny is not actually saying 'Rockbiter", but is saying the next line that follows. (00:16:40)

Repo! The Genetic Opera (2008)

Right before the end credits, as Grave Robber says "But Genco may survive if it undergoes surgery", right as Grave Robber says the word "may", his lips briefly don't match what is being said. (Confirmed in DVD commentary.).

Scary Movie 3 (2003)

When George is throwing up you can hear the vomit sound at the same time as he is spitting. (00:14:45)

Scream 2 (1997)

When Dewey is being stabbed up against the soundproof glass, you see a shot of Gale shouting "No." You can see a reflection of the killer in the glass standing motionless, but you can hear Dewey being stabbed. (01:18:45)

Showgirls (1995)

When Nomi is dancing at the Crave Club with the bouncer, she kicks him for making a suggestive comment and the bouncer stumbles backward into another guy on the dance floor. The bouncer tells the guy to "be cool", and the guy responds with "you be cool, buddy", but as we hear him say this, he's already punching the bouncer and his lips aren't moving along with the words. (00:17:35)

Shrek 2 (2004)

When the Fairy Godmother sings "Holding Out for a Hero" she tells the pianist to 'put it in C minor,' yet the pianist immediately begins to play in G minor, and the rest of the song is sung in that key. (01:08:15)

Source Code (2011)

This scene is repeated multiple times in the movie: usually when the main character enters the "source code" the scene begins by panning over a small pond showing a Canada goose taking flight. However the sound editor makes the mistake of dubbing in a recording of a hen mallard duck.

Speed (1994)

When Jack and Harry are running down the stairs to get to the elevator Harry radios his lieutenant and says "Mac we need more help up here now", but his mouth does not appear to be saying these words when it is visible.

Star Wars (1977)

When C-3PO lowers himself into the oil tub, as Luke says, "It just isn't fair." his head is shown from the side and he then turns his head away from the camera, but the words don't match the motion of his jaw (or his lips, if you look closely). (00:19:00)

When the Millennium Falcon is attacked after the group escape from the Death Star, there is a TIE fighter which makes an X-Wing sound.

When Vader and Tarkin learn that Leia has lied about the location of the Rebel base, we hear Darth say "I told you she would never consciously betray the rebellion." There is a pause and Vader continues to move. An obvious dubbing error.

Star Wars: Episode I - The Phantom Menace (1999)

Before the Trade Federation Droid Control Ship starts exploding from the inside, a Neimoidian says, "Nothing can get through our shield". But his mouth doesn't move until after he's said it. (01:57:45)

Star Wars: Episode III - Revenge of the Sith (2005)

After the buzz droids land on Obi-Wan's starfighter, Obi-Wan says, "I'm hit. Anakin?" As he says, "Anakin?" his head is turned to the side, but you can see that the last word doesn't quite fit his lips or the motion of his jaw. (00:05:10)

Star Wars: Episode V - The Empire Strikes Back (1980)

After Luke frees himself from the cave in the beginning, he stumbles towards the exit. You can hear his lightsaber go off, but it stays firmly on. Cut to him emerging, and now his lightsaber's off. (00:09:30)

Stargate (1994)

Right after Jackson has been dragged through the desert by the creature, it wakes him up and he says, "Get away from me," but his mouth never moves. (00:40:30)

Terminator 2: Judgment Day (1991)

John Connor's bike is an XR-100, it is a 4 stroke engine. In the movie they dub in the sound of a 2 stroke. It is a quiet little engine so that is why they probably dubbed in the sound. (00:32:00)

Thunderball (1965)

In the final chase, when Largo says 'Jettison cocoon,' his mouth does not match the words.

Tremors (1990)

Right after Bert kills the second graboid he gets on the radio and says "we killed that mother-humper". Val replies "...be advised there are two more mother-humpers". However Val's lips don't seem to be saying "humper". This occurs even in unedited versions of the film. (01:01:40)

V for Vendetta (2005)

When V says that he has never danced to any of the songs on his jukebox, a song is playing in the background, yet there is no record seen playing on the jukebox. This occurs even after V presses the button to activate the song.

The Wedding Singer (1998)

In the scene where Robbie is sitting outside and Linda walks up to him to tell him about why she called the wedding off, she firstly walks on the concrete and you can hear her footsteps, then she walks on the grass, but you can still hear her heels clicking.

West Side Story (1961)

During the opening overture, right when the orchestra starts "Maria", you can hear someone sneeze in the background. It's easier to hear on the soundtrack but you still can hear it in the movie.

Who Framed Roger Rabbit (1988)

In the secret room where Hoskins and Dolores are hiding Roger right before Hoskins hits his head on the lamp he says, "crazy

152

tunes," but his mouth doesn't move. (00:44:25)

The Wizard of Oz (1939)

When Dorothy, Scarecrow, and Tinman are in the forest where they find Lion, the first time Dorothy says "Lions and tigers and bears, oh my" her mouth doesn't move at first but when the camera cuts to the next shot her mouth finishes the phrase. (00:48:45)

CHARACTER
MISTAKES

Something a character wrongly states as fact, or spelling mistakes. Something more significant than a minor error anyone could make.

The Alamo (1960)

In a conference with Crockett and Bowie, Travis states that Fannin in Goliad is preparing to relieve the Alamo and will be ready to "march south by the end of the week." Goliad is 90 miles south of San Antonio. To relieve the Alamo, Fannin would need to march north.

Alien (1979)

When Ripley interfaces with Mother for the first time and sees the special order, an instruction reads as "Insure return of organism" rather than "Ensure return," a common enough grammatical error for humans but not one that a programmed supercomputer would generate.

American Pie (1999)

When Jim gets home and finds the apple pie on the counter with a note from his mother, the note reads "you're favorite", rather than "your". (00:31:40)

The Amityville Horror (2005)

When Lisa is taken to the hospital, she tells Kathy that she saw the ghost of Jodie DeFeo. The name of both of the DeFeo's daughters wasn't Jodie. Their names were Dawn and Allison. Jodie was the name of a demonic pig that the Lutz's daughter Missy had befriended.

Austin Powers: International Man of Mystery (1997)

Austin is supposed to be the archetypal Swinging Sixties Londoner yet he refers to his car as a Shaguar, a pun on 'Jaguar', pronouncing it 'Shag-war'. A native of this green and pleasant land would pronounce it 'Shag-u-ar', three syllables, not two, based on our pronunciation of the car manufacturer's name: Jag-u-ar.

Big (1988)

When Tom Hanks starts to play on the floor piano he throws the bag he is carrying aside and when he goes to leave he doesn't pick it up. He leaves it on the floor.

The Blind Side (2009)

When Coach Fullmer is recruiting Michael and SJ to Tennessee, he ends the conversation by calling SJ the wrong name - "my pleasure, CJ." (01:33:25)

Cadet Kelly (2002)

When Sir informs Kelly that she made the drill team, he says Captain Rigby instead of Major Rigby.

Clockstoppers (2002)

Early in the story Dr. Gibbs rationalises the story to come by using two cars traveling the road at greatly different speeds to illustrate "Einstein's theory of relativity". He basically says that the slower moving car seems to stand still as seen from the much faster car's point of view. But in real Einsteinian relativity, just the opposite happens. When two reference frames are traveling with respect to each other, each sees the other's time advancing more quickly.

The Dark Knight Rises (2012)

As Bruce Wayne is researching the jewel thief, the word "Heist" is spelled "Hiest" in a newspaper headline. (00:15:45)

Warner Bros. Pictures

The Day of the Jackal (1973)

Towards the end of the film the Jackal, in disguise as the fictional one-legged, grey haired Frenchman Andre Martin, finishes setting up his sniper's nest and removes his beret, revealing that he has only dyed his hair grey where it protruded. He has a circular mop of his normal chestnut brown hair under his hat! This is an incredibly stupid thing to do - it is a perfectly normal thing for a policeman (or any other security operative) to ask that someone showing identity papers remove his hat if he is wearing one. The Jackal is a professional assassin who meticulously prepares for all contingencies - he isn't going to throw away his whole plan for the sake of a bit of extra hair dye. (02:10:05)

Disturbia (2007)

In one scene, Ashley looks into Mr. Turner's yard with binoculars. She looks through the large glass circles. That would result in seeing everything smaller. If you want to see everything bigger, you are supposed to look through the small glass circles.

Flight (2012)

When Whip is in the hospital, standing straight in front of the camera is a ridiculous nurse; she takes down the empty IV bag and pulls the bag away from the IV line, she drops the bag on the floor, a big no-no, but try as she might she can't seem to get the spike to go into the new bag. While she's doing all this, she's waving that sterile spike everywhere, touching everything she can, including herself, and picking up germs that will go straight into Whip's IV line, and into his body, when, finally she gets that infected spike into the infected new bag.

Flight of the Phoenix (2004)

It's all very heroic and manly but the effort put into dragging the Phoenix into its takeoff position once the engine is started is totally wasted. Townes and A.J. are both experienced pilots and Elliott is supposedly a genius aeronautical engineer - they must surely be aware that the engine power required to taxi an aircraft is trivial compared to that required to lift it into the air. Even taking into account the drag of the skids and wheels, if that engine cannot propel the aircraft at a few kilometers an hour on the ground it cannot propel it to take off speed, nor keep it up once airborne. They are not there to steer the aircraft - they are taking the strain of the whole weight of the air-frame, dragging it into place, and the energy input of eight exhausted, underfed people would add nothing to the contribution of a 2500 bhp aircraft engine in moving the Phoenix. They are not trying conserve fuel - they had enough fuel for an extended flight with both engines at full throttle, so they have easily enough to run one engine throttled back to reduce stress on the air-frame, which they say they are going to do.

Full Metal Jacket (1987)

When the Marines are navigating through the Paris Island obstacle course, Hartman is shouting "It should take you no less than 10 seconds to negotiate this obstacle!" In other words, the LONGER it takes someone to get across, the better? (00:13:27)

Fury (2014)

On the way approaching town the camera pans to a woman's hanged body with a sign written in German around her neck. One of the crew asked Wardaddy what it said, to which he answered something like "It reads 'I am a coward who refused to fight for the German people'." That sign actually translates to "I wanted my children not to go fight" or Anglicized for better effect, "I refused to let my children to go to war." Interestingly, once into town, there appears the corpse of a hanged man with a sign written in German that does translate to what Wardaddy said of the first sign.

Gladiator (2000)

When Maximus is talking to Marcus Aerelius, he mentions that his wife has black hair. But in the scenes where we see her, she actually has brown hair. (00:24:40)

Prior to the opening battle, Quintus says "The danger to the calvary." instead of "cavalry." (00:04:00)

Gone with the Wind (1939)

When Melanie and Scarlett are talking with an (off-screen) wounded Confederate soldier, the soldier says he hasn't heard from his brother since Bull Run. Only Northerners refer to that battle as Bull Run; Southerners have always referred to it as Manassas.

Grease (1978)

When Frenchie is the only person remaining in the soda shop a guardian comes on and starts singing a song. While he is singing the song (toward the end of his singing) all the girls scatteringly head back toward the stairs. While they are walking up, one of the girls trips over her high heels. It is clearly shown, she's toward the front going around the back of the seat Frenchie is sitting in, around the round thing.

The Great Escape (1963)

The scene in the outdoor Parisian cafe is incredibly daft. First, the cafe owners call James Coburn's bizarrely-accented Australian to the telephone to keep him out of the way as their accomplices assassinate three uniformed German officers seated in the cafe in a drive by shooting. They then toast the killings with cognac, and that is the mistake - not the shootings, not the luring away of Coburn - the mistake is that the cafe proprietors celebrate the assassination of the German officers in broad daylight, in the open, without even stopping to think that such an action would have them shot, because all of this is done in the direct view of passers-by in broad daylight. Do they think those three German officers were the only ones in Paris? How did they know Coburn wasn't an undercover Gestapo agent or a French collaborator? Don't they stop to consider that in an occupied city machine gun fire is going to draw some attention from the authorities, who might just wonder what a couple of bullet riddled corpses are doing lying about the place?

Halloween II (1981)

The police claim the Myers house is at "45 Lampkin Lane." The address on the front porch clearly displays the number 709.

High School Musical 2 (2007)

Chad actually steps on first base before the baseman has the ball.

He was safe.

The Holiday (2006)

Arthur (who knew him) says that Cary Grant was from Surrey and Iris (who is from Surrey) agrees with him. Cary Grant was actually from Bristol.

In the last scene Iris hugs Olivia, saying, "Sophie, give us a kiss". (02:03:20)

Ice Princess (2005)

When Casey is using her knowledge of physics to advise a figure skater, she states, "Pull your arms in real tight. That increases your moment of inertia". In fact, this is the exact opposite of how it really works. Reducing her overall radius makes her rotational inertia smaller. (00:21:05)

Independence Day (1996)

In the Iraqi Desert, when the British soldiers speak of the casualties and losses, one of the British soldiers mentions the loss of the Belgian contingent and possible reinforcements, then makes a reference to the "Golan Straits"; there is no such place.

Jason Goes to Hell: The Final Friday (1993)

In the scene where they show Jason's mailbox, it says Vorhees. The correct spelling is Voorhees. (00:35:00)

John Wick: Chapter 2 (2017)

Once Santino and Ares find John again in the hall of mirrors, John is fighting two of the grunt men that came in with Ares and kills them. Both of which had light assault rifles and weapons on them. John and Ares proceed to empty their pistols out at each other before she runs off with Santino. John then throws his empty pistol away and gets up to pursue his target unarmed and while limping. It is unreasonable to think that someone with his skill and training and experience would not take two seconds to reach down and pick up one of the guns dropped by the two men he just killed before chasing after his target, especially given the highly trained body guard with him accompanying his target. As well as probable encounters with more grunts. To add to this, he was seen doing just this moments before when he had limited ammo and each time he'd down a few enemies he would pick up one of their guns and continue. (01:41:30)

Knight & Day (2010)

Outside Seville, Cruise jumps off a bridge on a stall with a sign that reads "Especial en sardines". This is senseless text. The correct spelling should be "Especialidad en sardinas".

London Has Fallen (2016)

When Mike and the SAS team leader first meet, the team leader introduces himself as Will Davis, Captain. However at the near end when they say goodbye to each other, Mike addresses him as Lieutenant. (01:07:35 - 01:25:35)

Mile 22 (2018)

During the opening raid of the FSB safe house, an operator is seen taking hard drives out of a safe. As he does, he states over the radio that they are "SSDs" (Solid State Drives), when in reality they are normal HDDs (Hard Disk Drives), which are noticeably larger than SSDs. (00:07:25)

Moana (2016)

When Maui and Moana set sail after defeating the Kakamora, Maui says they must head east. He turns the boat 90° as he says this. Throughout the next scene the setting sun is to the left of them (providing a beautiful backdrop to their fight), meaning that the boat must be heading north, not east.

The Pink Panther 2 (2009)

In the film, five items are stolen: the Magna Carta, the Turin Shroud, the Imperial Sword of Japan, the Pope's ring and the Pink Panther diamond. When Alfred Molina's character is challenged that they had found everything but the Pink Panther, he protests that 3 out of 4 is not bad, that's 75%. In fact, they had found 4 out of 5 or 80%.

Pitch Perfect (2012)

At the activities fair, after Benji and Jesse walk away from the Treblemakers, Bumper says "Let's match pitch." Then sings a note. The rest of the Treblemakers harmonize, rather than match the note that Bumper sings. (00:15:40)

In the scene where Becca and Jesse have a picnic, she tells Jesse that she knew Darth Vader was Luke's father, because "Vader literally means father in German." This is incorrect. However, it does mean father in Dutch. The German word for father is Vater.

Rambo: First Blood Part II (1985)

In the showdown scene between the Vietnamese officer and Rambo, the Vietnamese officer empties an entire magazine at Rambo from only about 20 metres away but only manages to hit the ground around Rambo's feet. What was he doing, aiming at his feet? He deserved to get blown up to bits for that effort.

Ray (2004)

When Ahmet is describing his idea for the song "The Mess Around" to Ray, he tells Ray the song is in G (major). However, Ray immediately plays the song in E flat major.

Runaway Train (1985)

When the front door of the old F-unit is refusing to open the guys put their shoulder to it. The door they are trying to bash outward actually swings into the area where they are standing. If they really wanted to go out that door they should have un-latched it and pulled.

Save the Last Dance (2001)

During the movie's opening credits, Sara is shown auditioning for Juilliard, which is misspelled as "Julliard" on a sign outside the room where the audition is occurring.

Scream 2 (1997)

During the scene in which they are all arguing whether or not film sequels are better than the original or not, someone says Sigourney Weaver's classic line from the movie Aliens: "Get away from her you bitch", and Randy makes a smart comeback and tries to correct him by saying "I think the correct line was 'stay away from her you bitch'. This is a film class, right?" Wrong - the first guy was right. This line is truly unconvincing for the Randy character, being a big movie buff and all. Jamie Kennedy decided to improvise as Joshua Jackson actually made the initial mistake by saying the wrong line, causing a different mistake.

Sex and the City 2 (2010)

In the scene where Carrie is printing an article she has written, the title reads: The Terrible Two's. A successful, educated writer would never have used an apostrophe to pluralize a word. Ever.

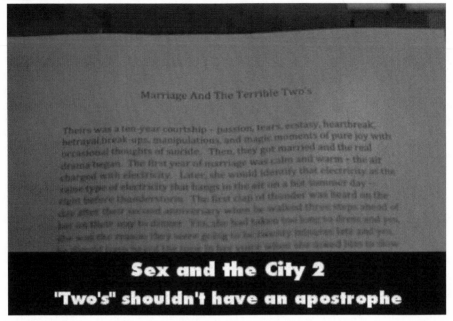

Sherlock Holmes (2009)

In the scene showing the outside of the hotel the British flag is flying upside down. The wider white band on the white X has to be top left next to the top of the flag pole. It is at the bottom, which is a universal distress sign.

The Social Network (2010)

At Henley, Prince Albert of Monaco is introduced as "His Royal Highness Prince Albert." He is a Serene Highness, not Royal. A British VIP would know the difference and say "His Serene Highness" instead.

Space Jam (1996)

When Stan inflates himself, Michael asks, "How'd he do that?", implying that he doesn't know the rules of the Looney Tunes world. Since Michael was rolled into a ball by the aliens earlier in the film, this shouldn't be too much of a surprise.

Speed (1994)

There is no way on earth that a police officer would shoot a hostage in the thigh to 'take them out of the equation'. Anyone who suggested such a thing would likely be taken out and shot themselves. Bullet wounds to the thigh are often fatal, as an injury to the femoral artery causes massive and frequently unstoppable blood loss. Breaking the femur often leads to fat embolisms as bone marrow gets into the bloodstream and then to the lungs. In fact a broken femur is a life threatening injury in itself, and a shattered femur - a typical bullet injury - would almost always result in a total amputation. You cannot aim carefully enough to avoid the bone or artery as their position in the body varies, (as will the bullet trajectory upon impact). Jack is an experienced cop and would know the potentially disastrous consequences of shooting someone in the thigh. He'd shoot him in the foot.

Spy Kids 3-D: Game Over (2003)

Before the Megarace, Rez looks back at the camera and says that they'll try to help him out-but you can see Juni's tires in front of Rez's car. In a shot before this one, Rez says Arnold will crush Juni-looking at the camera, which is in front of Rez.

Star Trek (2009)

When Chekov is discussing the plan to hide behind Saturn, he says, "...if Mr. Scott can get us to warp 4...". But on the viewscreen, it shows they are already traveling at warp 4.31. (01:34:40)

Star Trek II: The Wrath of Khan (1982)

While Khan is "interviewing" Chekhov and Terrell, he stated, "On Earth, two hundred years ago, I was a prince, with power over millions." The official date for this movie is 2285. That would place Khan on earth around 2085 by this statement.

However, it is made clear in the episode "Space Seed" that Khan and his followers escaped earth in the year 1996: nearly one hundred years earlier. Quite a way off to be a rounding error. (00:21:45)

Stuart Little 2 (2002)

In the football scene, when the kid boots the ball to George who is upfield, he then hits it at the other kid, who is also on his team. There are two problems here: 1) The original pass would have been offside, as you see the all of the other players are still charging up the pitch. 2) When George kicks the ball at the other boy's face, that would have been offside as well, for reasons that are stated above.

Swimming with Sharks (1994)

When Guy and his girlfriend are discussing why he loves the movies and how they help him remember important times in his life, Guy makes a reference to the obscure 1979 basketball movie The Fish That Saved Pittsburgh, and says how he loved Gabe Kaplan in it. Gabe Kaplan was never in The Fish That Saved Pittsburgh, but did star in a different obscure basketball movie from 1979 called Fast Break.

The Terminator (1984)

When Kyle steals the police officer's gun and asks him what the date is, the officer replies "12th, May, Thursday". The film is set in 1984. May 12th, 1984 was a Saturday.

Transcendence (2014)

The doctor diagnosing Will's illness tells Evelyn and Max that it's caused by "an isotope called polonium." Polonium is a chemical element, not an isotope. The word "isotope" refers to a form of an element (such as carbon-12 or carbon-14) not the element itself. It does not mean "radioactive substance", because many isotopes are stable. A doctor would know this. (00:17:00)

Underworld (2003)

On two occasions throughout the film, Kraven's accent changes - once when he is talking to Lucian near the beginning of the movie and near the end of the movie when he is telling Selene that Viktor killed her family.

Urban Cowboy (1980)

When Wes is drinking the tequila with the worm in it, he makes a toast to "la vida luna" and tells Sissy it's Spanish for "the crazy life". This is untrue, the correct Spanish translation for "the crazy life" is "la vida loca". "La vida luna" literally translates as "the life moon" or better yet "the moon life", but a more accurate translation is "the night life."

Vertical Limit (2000)

Those are the most haphazardly secured cases of nitro I've ever seen in a movie. Couldn't they spare a shoelace or duct tape to secure the top?

Where Eagles Dare (1968)

In the courtyard of the castle there is an anti-aircraft gun. You could probably not find a worse place for a gun like that even if you tried (except maybe if you put it inside, in a windowless room). In the position it is placed it can only fire at targets directly above the castle. What you want to do is fire at targets before they reach the castle. It would be better if they placed it on the roof, or even near the village below.

Without a Clue (1988)

Watson says that there are fifteen windows on the front of 221B Baker Street, but if you look, there are only twelve.

Witness (1985)

When Schaeffer, McFee, and Fergie walk down the dusty road to Amish village, Western gunslinger style, they make a silly mistake no cop would make - they assume that Amish villages are unarmed and undefended. No so. The Amish have no prohibition on guns and almost every house would have at least one hunting rifle or shotgun. The three bad guys are risking being shot to bits before they get halfway down that hill; they don't even make an attempt at concealment. (Wouldn't they also at least think John - a police officer - would still have his gun or might have got hold of a firearm from the Amish?)

The X-Files Movie (1998)

Mulder and Scully sneak into the morgue at Bethesda Naval Hospital to view the body of the dead fireman from the bomb blast. Mulder lifts the sheet back on the body to show that the man's tissue is "like jelly." Scully surmises there's been some kind of cellular breakdown, and then says the tissue is "completely edematous." However, Dr. Scully mispronounces "edematous" as ed-a-may-shuss. The correct pronunciation is i-dem-a-tuss. Being a doctor she'd know the difference. (00:37:45)

DELIBERATE
MISTAKES

Something definitely done deliberately (rather than by oversight), but which still results in a mistake. Rare.

Ace Ventura: Pet Detective (1994)

In the scene in which Ace is in the asylum, he breaks into a storage closet to view Finkle's belongings that were left behind when he escaped. At first the doorframe is such that the door closes against about an inch of wood, meaning the lock would be behind this wood, so Ace couldn't pry it open. In the closeup, the door's flush against the frame so Ace can use the sign to get between the door and the frame. In the wide shot it's back to how it was. (00:58:55)

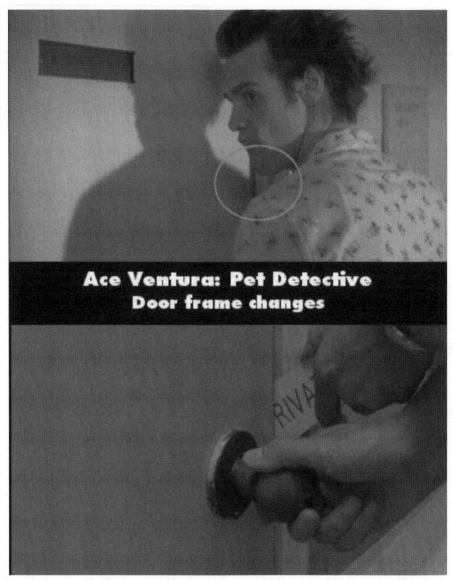

Warner Bros. Pictures

Alien (1979)

After Ash's body is incinerated, the interior walls of the Nostromo appear more metallic and grey than they were before. According to Ridley Scott, this was done deliberately to make the alien's presence appear more menacing.

Batman Returns (1992)

When the penguin goes into the cemetery, he bumps a tombstone and it moves. Almost certainly a tribute to legendarily poor director Ed Wood, who Tim Burton later directed a biopic of - this exact thing happened in one of his films. (00:39:15)

Beauty and the Beast (1991)

At the end of the film, Gaston shoots the Beast with an arrow and pushes the Beast out the window. When the Beast lands on the edge of the castle rooftop, the arrow has disappeared. Even if part of the arrow has broken off, a piece of it would still be in his back. [This, like many other incidents in the film, is a longtime Disney animated tradition. The company seems to believe that violence is less unpleasant if all evidence of it disappears quickly. This is why so many cuts seem to disappear or become less serious. The arrow vanishing is just another example.] (01:16:55)

When Gaston is in Belle's house and he puts his muddy boots on Belle's book, when she picks it up and it cuts, a white cloth magically appears in her hand to wipe off the mud. (00:17:40)

Beneath the Planet of the Apes (1970)

There are absolutely no lights ever to be found in the underground world and the ceiling is literally the surface's ground, but there is still a perfect level of lighting in the underground world regardless.

Beverly Hills Cop III (1994)

Twice in this film Axel is shot at by multiple gunmen using automatic weapons at close range - and they all miss. In the Earthquake theme ride the bullets ricochet of the rails at Axel's feet. Why are they all aiming low? Why don't they raise their aim? In the park outside he hides behind a perfectly ordinary park bench and the bullets hit the wooden slats. Not one goes through the open spaces between them? I know bad guys can't shoot straight in the movies, but this is ridiculous ...

The Big Lebowski (1998)

In the first bowling scene, all the lane numbers are backwards.

Category 7: The End of the World (2005)

When the New York subway is flooded the interior shot shows the station is Wilshire Blvd. Wilshire Blvd is in Los Angeles and the film clip appears to be stock footage from the Universal Studios Tour ride.

The Chronicles of Narnia: The Lion, the Witch and the Wardrobe (2005)

Obviously due to the family nature of the film, but when Peter stabs the White Witch's henchmen at battle, the sword always remains clean, and never bloody. (This is a Disney family film and as such no blood is shown. Still a mistake, but there's the reason). (01:56:10)

Final Destination 3 (2006)

There are a number of things wrong with the roller coaster scene (besides the obvious impossibility of a crash like this actually occurring): 1) The restraints use ratchets to lock, not hydraulics. A coaster of this type wouldn't even have any hydraulic lines. 2) No roller coaster has restraints that lower by themselves. 3) The attendants didn't check all the restraints. This is ALWAYS necessary, on ANY ride. 4) On any roller coaster, the Dispatch button (or "Start" in the movie) must be held down until the train is clear of the station. This is a safety feature to make sure the attendants are clear of the moving train. If the button is released before the train is clear of the station, it will stop. 5) At the bottom of the lift, the lift chain curves to follow the track into the station. This is impossible, a lift chain cannot curve horizontally, only vertically (normally at the top of the hill).

Finding Nemo (2003)

Towards the end of the movie fish are seen to swim down in order to submerge the net in which they have been caught. Although the attempt seems logical, it actually needs power against the net to push it down. None of the fish seem to touch the net at the bottom however and if it is the whole mass of fish achieving it, then the bottom fish should have been squashed against the net which (again) isn't the case. 'What brings the net down?' is the question here. (Done deliberately by Disney/Pixar to be visually aesthetically pleasing.)

When Dory is inside the whale, she doesn't have the scars from the jellyfish sting anymore. [This is actually a long-standing Disney tradition. The company seems to believe that it is less traumatic to see violence onscreen if the evidence is gone immediately (blood, scars, etc. always disappear). Still an error, but it wasn't the fault of the CGI animators.] (01:09:30)

Jon Sandys

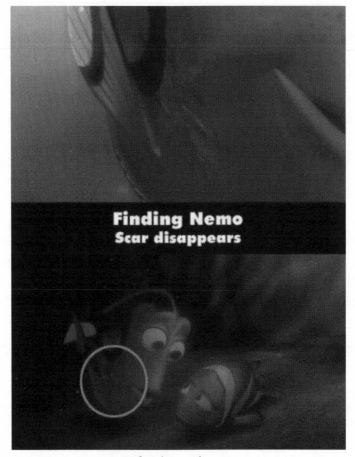

Walt Disney Pictures

Get Smart (2008)

When Max and 99 are in the air, they can be seen talking to each other. This is not possible (as proven on Mythbusters) even if you were yelling at the top of your lungs. The wind would make any noise unrecognizable, yet we hear them talking to each other just fine.

Gladiator (2000)

The historically inaccurate portrayal of stirrups in the film was actually due to the stuntmen enacting the cavalry charge in the initial battle scene. Apparently the stuntmen refused to ride the horses over the forest terrain at full gallop without stirrups because it was far too dangerous for both horse and rider. (Galloping a horse through forest or any uneven terrain is incredibly dangerous.) Stirrups were granted as a concession to the stuntmen on the grounds of saftey. Since they were included in this scene, the film makers decided to allow them in all other scenes where necessary. (Only seven stuntmen were used in the filming of these scenes - all the other riders are just CGI copies.)

The Great Santini (1979)

After having wrestled with Santini in his office, Col. Virgil Hedgepath tells Santini, "And no more assaulting corporals in the latrine." Marines use the naval term "head" in refering to the restroom, and would never call it "the latrine." However, since "latrine" is better known to civilians, this could be a deliberate mistake by the film makers.

Harry Potter and the Chamber of Secrets (2002)

When bars are placed on Harry's windows, so he does not escape, it is apparent that his windows have complete leaded panes of glass. Yet when Harry is being rescued, Ron and Harry speak with each other, even in low voices, through his visibly closed windows. (00:08:00 - 00:09:00)

Ice Age 4: Continental Drift (2012)

Manny refers to the pirate rabbit as the Easter Bunny, even though Easter never existed in prehistoric times. (00:33:55)

The Interpreter (2005)

When the Matoban delegation arrives at the UN, it shows the motorcade entering the circle in front of the UN Secretariat building and stopping at the revolving doors right at the front the staff entrance. Diplomats' motorcades always continue on to the delegates' entrance under a protective tent in front of the GA building so as to allow VIPs to alight from their vehicles to prevent potential snipers from having a view of them. The very next shot of the ambassador shows him riding the escalator, which is at the delegates' entrance, going up to the General Assembly building. This would not have been possible unless they made him walk about 300 meters outside in broad daylight. No chance of that seeing he was already being protested on 2nd avenue all the way from the Queensboro bridge. Obvious reason for this error: The shot of the delegation getting out of the cars looks far better in the open right in front of the UN secretariat building rather than inside a protective tent.

Jeepers Creepers 2 (2003)

When the Creeper gets stabbed throught the eye with the javelin, it goes through the front of his eye, but when it comes out the other end the eye is facing backward. (00:50:00)

The Lego Movie (2014)

In the scene where Emmet drives to work, you get Emmet's view of the dashboard with his hand switching on the radio. The car at that moment has no front window, perhaps to make the car look bigger from the inside. (00:04:50)

The Lion King (1994)

At the elephant graveyard, little Simba claws Shenzi in the face. When Mufasa saves Simba from the hyenas, the cuts are gone, a few seconds later. [This was done intentionally, I'm sure, for two reasons. The first being, Disney doesn't let fresh scars linger on the screen too long. Secondly, during that same scene when Mufasa rescues Simba & Nala, he claws Banzai in the rear. To stress the point later in the movie, that severe scar is shown too, but only briefly, it too disappears because of reason 1. Still a "mistake", but there's why.] (00:21:50)

Buena Vista

The Lord of the Rings: The Fellowship of the Ring (2001)

In the Chamber of Mazarbul, when Legolas lets loose the double arrows at the Troll near Balin's Tomb, in that shot he stands in front of the same wall as in the next shot. In this second shot he spins around, slices two Orcs and then looks at the Troll in front of him, only this second shot is flipped. In those two shots he stands in front of a solid rock wall with particular markings between two pillars. In the next shot it shows Legolas' back and the Troll down below as Legolas ducks down avoiding the Troll's chain flying overhead. Then in the next consecutive shot from the front again Legolas rises and is now standing in front of a stone wall that has a large alcove with books also between two pillars. These shots were spliced from a longer sequence because the two walls noted are adjacent to each other - in the film the alcove wall is to the left of the solid wall and they share a pillar between them. (00:30:30)

The Lord of the Rings: The Return of the King (2003)

When Théoden and the Rohirrim ride out of camp, as Éomer shouts, "Form up! Move out!" and in the following close-up when Théoden shouts, "Ride! Ride now for Gondor!" please note that Théoden's sheath is at his left side and Éomer's strap hangs down his left shoulder to his right side - whereas normally they are the opposite way. Both shots are flipped for direction continuity. (01:49:30)

After Théoden shouts, "Make safe this city!" in the flipped close-up of Éomer, as he reacts to the approaching Mûmakil, his sheath and helmet straps are both noticeably backwards. (00:31:40)

Just after we hear Gandalf shout, "Get the women and children out! Get them out! Retreat!" there is a flipped shot of many soldiers with their swords at their right side, as some run through the gate being held open by others. (00:22:40)

After entering the Tower of Cirith Ungol, Sam runs down a passageway and looks up and in the next shot he starts to run up the stairs. These two shots are flipped as things on his body are backwards. (02:20:10)

The Lord of the Rings: The Two Towers (2002)

Just after they've clashed with the Warg, while riding on Arod, Legolas lets loose his first arrow and hits a Warg in his face and it flips over. In this first shot, the background behind this Warg is the same background as in the very next shot. This first background shot is really the successive shot of this second background shot. The shot just after Gimli falls off his horse, is the third successive shot, only it's been flipped. The same men on horses are riding across the field in the background, as this was one piece of footage that was cut into three parts. Warg and riders were added to the image, to make them appear different and one was flipped. (00:11:05)

During the Warg battle, the fourth shot after the close-up of Legolas letting loose the arrow while riding on Arod, a Warg and rider attack a Rohan. In the background is a particular hillside with some dead bodies, and on the left of the screen lies a dead horse with an arrow in its rear. The very next shot, a horse and rider fall and a Warg attacks the rider. The background hillside in this shot, dead horse and all, is the same background plate as the previous one, only it's been flipped. (00:11:05)

Lost Treasure (2003)

The four main "good guy" characters are stuck on an island with people who are trying to kill them. Steven Baldwin's character brings a pistol and takes a machine gun from one of the bad guys. Several times they overcome other armed men, but after defeating them, never bother to take the bad guys' guns. At one point, two characters argue over who gets to carry the pistol, yet when they knock out a man armed with a rifle, they leave it with him and just walk away.

The Martian (2015)

The atmosphere on Mars is only 1% as dense of that as Earth, so 175kph windstorms would feel like a light breeze. They would have very little effect on the astronauts or MAV. The writers of the book and the film were aware of this, it was a small cheat to let the rest of the story unfold.

The Matrix (1999)

In the rooftop fight scene where Neo unloads 2 pistols at an agent and misses, you can hear the guns firing from behind, followed by 2 clicks suggesting that the clips are empty. Neo's guns are both semi-automatics and would therefore not click when empty as the slides would be locked back after the final shot. The click sounds were obviously added later to indicate to viewers that his clips were empty. (01:46:15)

Meet the Spartans (2008)

During the scene of the Spartans moving out, they sing "I Will Survive." Sonio is clearly singing the song alone, because his lips are singing the song before the music or anyone else is singing.

Miller's Crossing (1990)

When the two assassins enter Leo's bedroom and try to gun him down, the one on the right has left his tan overcoat open. He's the one that escapes from Leo initially. Shortly thereafter, Leo guns him down, firing up into a second story window. At this point we see that the assassin's coat is now buttoned up, probably to conceal the numerous squibs used in his death scene. (00:41:00)

Miss Congeniality 2: Armed and Fabulous (2005)

As "Fake Dolly" runs away from Gracie, it is rather obvious in the shot facing Dolly as she runs down the stairs and then when she turns to look behind her, that it really is a fake Dolly running.

(00:48:20)

Monsters, Inc. (2001)

When Boo laughs repeatedly while playing hide-n-seek with Sully in the men's room, nothing happens to the electricity - no surges as with all other times she laughs. [In the audio commentary by the directors, they explained that it would've been distracting if an energy surge occurred every time Boo laughed, so they simply didn't address the issue. A reasonable course of action, but still a mistake.] (00:37:30)

Mr. Deeds (2002)

Am I REALLY supposed to believe that a helicopter is capable of hovering above the top of Mt Everest? [In the DVD specials, the filmmakers say that they're absolutely aware that it's not possible for a helicopter to hover above Mt Everest. They just thought it would be a funny scene if a helicopter pulled the dead guy away from the mountain.] (00:02:15)

On Her Majesty's Secret Service (1969)

Blofeld doesn't recognize James Bond in this film, even though they met face-to-face in the previous movie, "You Only Live Twice." There is a production-related reason for this. Ian Fleming wrote "On Her Majesty's Secret Service" in 1963 (in which Bond and Blofeld met for the first time), and he wrote "You Only Live Twice" in 1964. However, "You Only Live Twice" was adapted for film first (in 1967), and "On Her Majesty's Secret Service" was adapted afterward (in 1969). Because the 1969 film was so faithful to its source material, Blofeld and Bond are basically meeting for the first time...again. The producers were aware of this continuity problem and intended to have James Bond undergo plastic surgery for "On Her Majesty's Secret Service" (which would conveniently explain Blofeld not recognizing him, as well as the fact that Sean Connery had been replaced by George Lazenby in the lead role). But the plastic surgery idea was discarded in faithfulness to the novel, resulting in a glaring continuity problem between the 1967 and 1969 films.

P.S. I Love You (2007)

After the broken suspender clasp smacks Gerry in the face, in the close-up it lands under the dresser, within the wide strip of light reflection. In all other shots the entire area beneath the dresser is in shadow. (00:11:00)

Pearl Harbor (2001)

It's 1941 in a military base and no one is smoking...

Peter Pan (2003)

After Peter says, "We can't both have her lady," he shuts the window from the outside and the bottom pane is placed on the outside of the top stained glass pane. This is obviously done specifically for this shot so Peter would be able to shut the window and try to keep the Darlings from opening it. However, in the next shot as the Darlings succeed in opening the 'stuck' window, the bottom pane is on the inside of the top stained glass pane. (00:02:05 - 00:58:45)

John yells, "I've got it! I've got it!" jumps onto his bed and we see the length of John's one blanket, mattress and bed frame near the other furniture. In the next two shots as John runs across his bed, the blanket at the foot of the bed is not only pulled all the way out, using what hung over the foot of the mattress in the previous shot, but another blanket is added for extra length. Most blatantly apparent is the span of this mattress and bed frame, to increase the running distance, in relation to the furniture around it. (00:21:35)

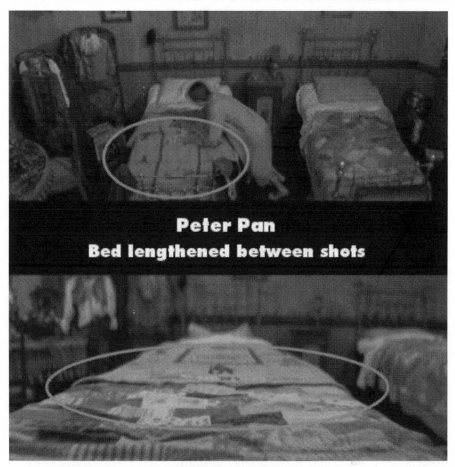

Universal Pictures

Pirates of the Caribbean: On Stranger Tides (2011)

When Jack fights the impostor, they are roughly the same height, but when the impostor is revealed to be Angelica, she is suddenly much shorter than him. (00:21:30 - 00:23:50)

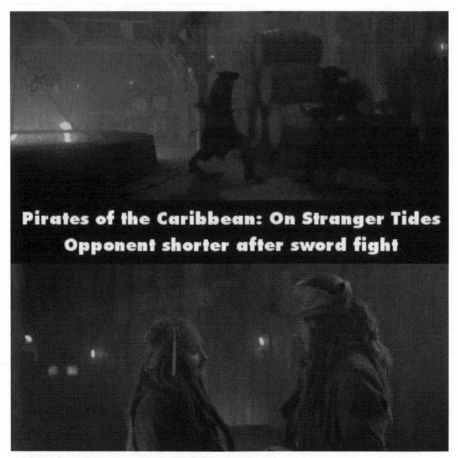

Walt Disney Pictures

Pirates of the Caribbean: The Curse of the Black Pearl (2003)

The East India Trading Company in reality, branded pirates with a 'P' on their foreheads, never on their arms, the way Captain Jack has it. It was deliberately decided to be historically inaccurate, feeling it looked better on Depp's arm. (Confirmed on commentary.) (00:17:20)

When Jack Sparrow and Will Turner take a rowboat and put it over their heads upside-down and walk on the bottom of the harbor (about 20 feet deep by the looks of it), wouldn't the rowboat rise to the surface? The amount of air trapped in the boat appears to be around 3-5 cubic meters, even at three that would provide plenty of lift to lift a boat twice that size and both people to the surface. This isn't even taking into account that wood and people are both fairly buoyant in and of themselves, even without the air pocket to aid. This scene is a direct homage to an earlier pirate movie, The Crimson Pirate, in which three characters do the same thing, hence this is a deliberate mistake.

Keira's stunt double Sonia is obvious in different shots throughout the film. When Elizabeth walks onto the deck of the Pearl, only to see the skeletal pirates, she stumbles backward and lands on the tarp, and it's very apparent that the one who comes back down from mid-air onto the tarp and goes back up is Sonia. Later on Isla de Muerta, Elizabeth whacks Jacoby (burning beard) with the gold rod and soon after she approaches a second pirate. This pirate is very pleased with himself when he takes the gold bowl off his head, and we can then see it is Sonia actually whacking him, but in the very next shot it is Keira reacting to whacking the guy. (00:59:05 - 02:00:05)

After Barbossa takes the apple from Jack and throws it into the water, the sailing Interceptor is shown. Out on the edge of the bow are two men. One is dressed as Will, but it is neither Orlando nor his body double, Mark. The man behind Will is obviously not one of Jack's crew either. (01:21:15)

Platoon (1986)

Throughout the entire movie, every time Charlie Sheen is not wearing his helmet, especially when he's out in the field in this tropical climate, his hair is always meticulously combed back, blow-dried and puffy. As a veteran, I know from personal experience that when you take your helmet off, especially in a climate like that, the reality is your hair will be messy, sweaty, pressed flat and most unattractive.

Jon Sandys

Scooby-Doo (2002)

In the first scene Velma gets sprayed by the hose and slips but gets her foot caught on the chain; hanging upside down, but her skirt doesn't go "up". Deliberate to maintain the "family movie" tone. (00:02:40)

Spy Kids 3-D: Game Over (2003)

After the game has entered the real world, and Floop and Minion are there to "save the day", Carmen and Juni throws seven pairs of glasses to them. But afterwords, we see there are only four pairs of glasses on Minion and one pair on Floop, which totals five. (01:11:10)

Star Trek: Generations (1994)

After the trilithium missile hits the sun, it is shown going out in real time from Veridian III. As the planet is relatively earth-like, it is several light-minutes away from the sun. The filmmakers wanted it to be obvious that the missile was successful, so they ignored the speed of light. (01:20:35)

Star Wars (1977)

After the Tusken Raider has attacked Luke, he raises his stick over his head and shouts. The movement of his clothing is extremely unnatural. During the editing, they put the same footage forward, then backward many times, to add emphasis to his movements, but it looks decidedly odd. (00:29:02)

When Obi Wan deactivates the Death Star's force field, there's an electronic gauge going down and a sign in clear English with the word POWER - as we've seen in shuttles and other places, they don't use English. The studio decided it was better to show "power" and "tractor beam" in English so that the audience would know what Obi-Wan was doing. The lettering we see in Jedi doesn't really affect the plot, so it doesn't need to be English. Still doesn't really fit though. This is fixed on the DVD.

20th Century Fox

Superman Returns (2006)

When Lex tests the crystal fragment, it knocks out all the power on the airplane Lois is flying in, yet the flight attendant's amplified voice can still be heard over the speakers. (00:30:40)

Taxi 2 (2000)

When the Evo crashes into the tanks it jumps into them at height but there was nothing there to make the car jump. (01:17:25)

Top Gun (1986)

In the shot where the F-14 and F5 canopies are only 3-feet apart, you can see that the writing on the side of MAVs F-14 is backwards. Also, if the F-14 was inverted, with the sun more-or-less above, its cockpit would be in shadow, not with sunlight on the nose, as seen. (00:08:55)

Toy Story (1995)

When Buzz Lightyear demonstrates his "flying" abilities in front of the other toys, his left wing would have clipped the car track entering the loop-de-loop, and the right wing would have hit the track when leaving the loop. (00:18:50)

Toy Story
Buzz's wings wouldn't fit through the loop

Buena Vista

Transformers (2007)

If you pay extremely close attention to the scene of all of the Decepticons responding to the small Transformer's message regarding the location of the Allspark, notice that the shot of the police car and the fake helicopter pilot are duplicate shots used earlier in the film.

Troy (2004)

During the Trojan attack on the Greeks at the beach, before Hector and "Achilles" have at it, there are two separate close-ups of Hector's sword slicing across a man's face, who promptly spins around and spews blood. This particular man is enjoyed twice in two takes of the same shot, just before and after Odysseus' close-ups. Then as if that's not enough, a few shots later this spewing man is actually seen a third time, but this time from another angle. (01:42:30)

X-Men 2 (2003)

Where did Storm's accent go? The accent she had in X-Men 1 is completely gone in X-Men 2.

OTHER MISTAKES

Any other kind of mistake.

101 Dalmatians (1996)

When the nanny comes home with the tags, they call Jewel to get hers first. Jewel has a penis.

12 Rounds (2009)

At 1:39:14 the bomb arms, 32 seconds later at 1:39:46 (two seconds after it should have blown up) Dan and Molly jump from the helicopter. Then 10 secs later at 1:39:56, the plane FINALLY blows up after giving them those extra 12 secs to jump and conveniently make it to the pool below.

Ballistic: Ecks vs. Sever (2002)

In the scene where Ecks is chasing Sever, you see Ecks put a shell into an open chambered shotgun. This means that there is only one shell in the gun. A moment later when he yells stop inside the building he cocks the gun again. Thus, he is holding up Sever without any shells in the gun.

Bambi (1942)

After the great fire scene there is a raccoon that drags her baby to shore and begins cleaning it. A few seconds later the baby has jumped across to the other side of his father and siblings, but the mother does not stop licking.

Basic (2003)

When Connie Nielsen is driving the Hummer (with John as the passenger), the steering wheel doesn't move, but her hands do.

The Boondock Saints (1999)

When Rocco taunts the Russians he is punched in the face, yet he continues talking in a steady tone, and finishes his joke while falling into the bar. (00:20:39)

Braveheart (1995)

When Robert the Bruce returns to the battlefield at Falkirk, there are 2 children supposedly crying over a loved one. If you look at the blonde girl she is actually laughing. (02:12:00)

Bullitt (1968)

During the big chase scene, a car hits a camera right after it passes a blue '68 GTO.

Charlie Wilson's War (2007)

In Wilson's Congressional office, the Texas flag on his left is mounted upside down. The white panel belongs on the top of the flag, not the bottom.

Charlie's Angels (2000)

At one stage the Angels speak with each other in a different language, so that the people sitting next to them wouldn't understand. Having listened to it for a few times, I realized it was Finnish. Funny though, the thing they actually said there (in Finnish), was totally different than the written translation. (00:41:45)

As the girls learn about their assignment from Charlie, he shows them a film. The film shows Knox in a tree. His sweatshirt says "BOSTON" in white letters. It is backwards in that shot, and the scene following. (00:13:34)

CHIPS (2017)

Near the start of the movie Jon indicates that he has titanium in his right arm, but towards the end of the movie the bullet ricochets off his left arm. (00:08:55 - 01:34:45)

Clue (1985)

In one of the first scenes in the study, Mr. Boddy hands each guest a weapon and then proceeds to turn out the lights. The room is thrown into complete darkness. Unfortunately, there is a roaring fire in the fireplace that would have illuminated the room enough for everyone to see what was going on.

Clueless (1995)

When Josh and Cher are driving home from a party, they show a shot of the car. It's a blue sports car that passes a Hertz car rental sign. When Elton is driving Cher home from the party in the Valley, they show the exact same shot of the blue sports car passing the Hertz car rental sign.

The Color Purple (1985)

Mister cooks Shug Avery a breakfast of grits, biscuits and ham, and takes it to her room. She throws the breakfast against the wall. The breakfast leaves a bright yellow and bright red stain on the wall. There was nothing on the tray that could have left those colors on the wall. (00:51:10)

Die Another Day (2002)

The underground station is supposed to have been abandoned long ago, and there is ancient advertising for Ford cars on the wall. But in the entranceway to the platform there's a recent ad for Philips electronics. (00:58:55)

Die Another Day
Modern advert in abandoned old station

MGM Pictures

Die Hard 2 (1990)

The female journalist is called Samantha Coleman through the movie, but appears in the credits as Samantha Copeland.

Django Unchained (2012)

When we see the "regulators" riding over the hill on the way to kill Django and Schultz, if you look carefully at the right-center portion of screen, you can see one of the stuntmen fall off his horse and the horse continues to run down the hill without him. To make matters even worse, it appears the stuntman rolls right in front of another horse and gets trampled. (00:41:00)

Drive (2011)

In the pre-credit scenes when the chopper spots the runaway car, Driver guns it (he clenches his jaw, fists and you hear the engine revving and gears changing) but he never catches up with the two cars only a few feet in front of him (which are proceeding at normal speed) for the whole length of the bridge.

Dude, Where's My Car? (2000)

When Chester is taking Jacko's pipe, Nelson gets up out of his seat. When they show Jacko really really mad, you can look in the background and Nelson is sitting down. When they show him again he is out of his seat.

Dunkirk (2017)

When the pilot of the Spitfire is shown ditching into the water, his engine is windmilling at high RPM as he impacts the water. This would have resulted in all of the prop blade tips being bent backwards; however, as it shows him trying to escape the sinking airplane, the prop blades are perfectly straight.

Fantastic Voyage (1966)

During the miniaturizing scene the technicians controlling the forklift wore sterile gloves, the nurses assembling the syringe did not.

The Goonies (1985)

With Andy weighing at least 100 lbs, surely Troy and the guys trying to pull "her" up would notice that a bucket carrying the sweater is nowhere near the weight of a person. Even if they filled it with coins from the wishing well, it still wouldn't come close to the weight of an actual person, regardless of how idiotic and pompous Troy and his two friends are.

Halloween 2 (2009)

When Laurie has her episode in the bathroom about killing Annie, the clock stays at 7:03 the whole time.

Halloween: Resurrection (2002)

After Michael kills Laurie at the beginning, he hands the knife to the inmate with the clown mask. The next kill is the cameraman for which he uses the tripod ends. A few scenes later they show Michael standing holding a knife with fresh blood on it. He hasn't killed anybody with this knife yet so where did the blood come from?

Hannibal (2001)

When Clarice is reading the letter from Hannibal, we hear a voice over, however what he says differs from what the letter says, specifically the "your good friend" before the signature, which Hannibal says, but which isn't in the letter. (00:35:35)

Happily N'Ever After (2006)

While the wizard is speaking near the portal, a ghost image of him appears to the left.

Home Alone (1990)

Kevin rides down the stairs on his sled and out the door. He originally lined up the sled at the top of the stairs, but it is clear that the stairs lie to the right of the door. His sled went straight down the stairs, therefore making it impossible to go straight out the door in one movement as shown. (00:25:25)

Home Alone 2: Lost in New York (1992)

In the scene where Kevin is making the hotel reservation on the phone, the lady does not even ask the dates of when he will be arriving and leaving the Plaza.

The Hunger Games (2012)

The video stream displayed in the night sky showing which tributes have died after the first day does not add up correctly. They display in district order. We see the start, the girl from three (so the boy is still alive), and the boy from four with no breaks. Then they break away to show Katniss and the control room, after which they continuously show the boy and girl from seven, the boy from eight (so the girl is still alive), the girl from nine (so the boy is still alive), and then fade to the end. We know that Foxface, the girl from five, dies later in the movie. Even if we assume that during the portion not shown, the girl from four, the boy from five, and both tributes from six are dead, that's only a total of ten. Thirteen are supposed to be dead at that point in the movie. (01:16:20)

Independence Day (1996)

When the huge alien ship settles over the White House there is an exterior wideshot of the grounds. At the bottom of this shot it's funny how there are many tourists - adults and children, just milling around in front of the gate and across the street with a van driving along between the two sides, and not one has any sort of reaction to the alien ship. This real shot of the White House (some shots had smaller-scale models) had the CG ship edited in during post production. (Visible on fullscreen DVD.)

Independence Day
Huge alien ship gets no reaction from tourists

20th Century Fox

Kong: Skull Island (2017)

Throughout the film Mason goes through all sorts of shenan-igans - explosions, fire fights, falling off a cliff, almost drowning, this woman really goes through the wringer. It's a bit surprising then, that at the very end of the film when the good guys finally come to the rescue that she looks like she has just finished pos-ing for a shampoo commercial with not a hair out of place.

The Lord of the Rings: The Fellowship of the Ring (2001)

When the hobbits are hiding under the tree trunk from the Ring-wraith in the beginning, you can see space to the left and right of the tree above them. Logically when the Ringwraith walks past the tree you would see it on the right side of the tree first, then on the left, but you don't - it looks like it walks out of the tree instead of behind it. [Confirmed on the commentaries - Elijah Wood asks his fellow actors if anyone spotted the mistake: 'It kind of magically comes out of the tree'. Sean Astin: 'You mean it doesn't pass from the other side?' Wood: 'No, it comes out from the centre.'] (00:51:40)

The Lord of the Rings: The Two Towers (2002)

It seems as though the Elves at the battle of Helm's Deep aren't quite as coordinated and elegant as Elves are rumoured to be. During the Helm's Deep battle scene, Aragorn is shouting com-mands to the Elven archers. In the close up shot of Aragorn while it's still raining, look to the left of Aragorn, there is an Elf who gets hit in the head by the quivers on the back of the Elf next to him. (01:04:50)

At the battle of Helm's Deep, Theoden, Aragorn, Legolas and the rest ride out of the Keep to meet the enemy, watch as the first men out of the gate kill all the Uruks on the bridge, yet the men riding behind them continue to hack and slash away at thin air.

(02:38:30)

Mask (1985)

When Rocky is in the funhouse looking at himself, he appears to look relatively "normal". But it's very obvious that it's got nothing to do with the mirror, and more to do with the removal of a lot of makeup. For example, Rocky usually has almost no nose, but in the mirror he has Eric Stoltz's very well developed nose.

Midway (1976)

Another "Recycled Footage Segment" via Tora! Tora! Tora!: When 3 Officers on Midway come out of their bunker and say that the runway is still operational, the footage of the B-17 with the landing gear problem mentioned elsewhere is blatantly used.

Mommie Dearest (1981)

When Joan is cutting up her rose garden, she is ranting and raving about how mad she is at Mayer, and how they're calling her box office poison. But if you look closely at her lips, they aren't moving.

The Mummy Returns (2001)

When Rick and Ardeth Bay save Evie from the warehouse after Imhotep is resurrected, there are four mummies chasing them when they get on the double-decker bus. Rick shoots one of the mummies and "kills" it. He shoots another one in half and goes to the top of the bus to fight another one. The top portion of the mummy that got shot in half then fights Ardeth Bay. Evie kills the mummy that got shot in half and the top part of the bus gets torn off by the bridge and kills the mummy Rick is fighting. John stops the bus and they all sign with relief. Whatever happened to the fourth mummy chasing them? (00:43:20 - 00:46:40)

Old School (2003)

When Mitch, Frank, and Beanie decide that they are going to have a party they say the party is on a Friday night. When they show the outside of Mitch's house you see the sign for the party and it says the party is on Thursday at 9:00. Then when Frank talks to the guys with the beer bong he says that tomorrow he has a nice Saturday planned. If the sign is right then he would have a pretty nice Friday.

Passport to Paris (1999)

In the beginning of the movie, when you first see Mary-Kate (aka Mel) and Ashley (aka Ally), Mary-Kate walks off without ever closing her locker.

Pirates of the Caribbean: The Curse of the Black Pearl (2003)

Pintel and Ragetti fire the chain link cannonball, and it hits the square rigged mast aboard Interceptor. There's a shot of two men falling from the top of the mast, just before Interceptor's mast crashes onto the Pearl. They are not part of Jack's crew, who are all accounted for aboard the Pearl later. The only one of Jack's crew to die is the Asian man, when he's stabbed by a pirate and falls overboard. Nor can they be Barbossa's crew, because they haven't boarded yet. (01:27:00)

Rampage (2018)

Davis tells Kate to go and she jumps out of the falling plane, her chute opening. Davis then takes a minute to free Harvey from the plane as it's still falling before they both get out. Once they are free falling he takes a few seconds before he pulls their chutes as well. However as they are coming down close to the plane crash site, Kate is near level with them in altitude as they are all coming down together. With how high she was when she jumped out compared to the time it took for Davis and Harvey to get out of the plane and open their chutes, she would have been several minutes behind them in the sky, not right next to them. (00:47:45 - 00:49:05)

Resident Evil: Afterlife (2010)

Pretty much everyone in the film, especially Alice, seems to be able to fire their weapons without reloading at all.

Rudolph, the Red-Nosed Reindeer (1964)

At the end of the show when the misfit toys are being delivered, the elf in Santa's sleigh gives an umbrella to each of the misfits so they can glide down with the exception of the bird, who jumps off, apparently forgetting that he is a misfit toy and can't fly; as he stated earlier in the show, he can only swim.

Saving Silverman (2001)

When Judith is locked in J.D. and Wayne's basement, she is first wearing a long night gown and she is chained at the ankle to an engine. Then she is given a box of clothes to use and she is next seen wearing shorts - how did she put them on if she was chained at the ankle? (00:45:10)

The Secret of my Success (1987)

When Michael J. Fox is in the pool with Auntie Vera, she pulls off his shorts, however you can clearly see the flesh-coloured pants he has on underneath.

Shane (1953)

During the final shootout in the saloon, young Joey yells, "Shane, look out!" Alan Ladd whirls around and his gun goes off. But the gun isn't pointed anywhere near the bad guy who is standing on the second floor balcony. Shane more than likely shot the furnace that was off to the right. Yet, the bad guy still manages to do a face plant on the barroom floor.

Sixteen Candles (1984)

The chunk of hair that Ted has in the car is in a ponytail, and much longer than the hair cut off in the door.

Sneakers (1992)

Towards the end where they steal the chip, they are detected and about a million security guards are all running around, yet 30 seconds later, the only security guard is one man with a shotgun. What happened to their big army of security guards? (01:41:30 - 01:42:55)

Son of the Mask (2005)

It was established in the first Mask that the mask does not work in the daytime, but it works during the day in this movie.

South Park: Bigger, Longer & Uncut (1999)

When the switch is thrown to electrocute Terrence and Phillip, it's pulled downwards. A few shots later, we see Cartman jump in to save T and P by turning the switch off. He also pulls the switch downwards instead of pushing it upwards. (01:06:05)

Spy Kids 3-D: Game Over (2003)

Towards the end of the movie, Carmen hands a guy some 3D glasses with a crack in one of the lenses and says something like "Sorry it's the last one," but less than a minute later hands a different guy a pair of 3D glasses.

Star Wars (1977)

During the scene when Obi-Wan is sneaking around the Imperial ship, a group of stormtroopers march by in a close group. One of the troopers is losing his armour and is attempting to hold it on.

Star Wars: Episode II - Attack of the Clones (2002)

After getting off the airspeeder at Naboo Padme and Anakin walk down a long balcony. R2D2 behind them has a huge dent visible on his dome. How did that happen? Did he fall down the stairs at some point? (00:39:10)

Star Wars: Episode III - Revenge of the Sith (2005)

To escape from the elevator, Anakin cuts a hole in the ceiling. Later, when they rescue the Chancellor, they almost get crushed by another elevator (it is another one. Each elevator has a number. Obi Wan said the number of this elevator before and it was different than the one that had the hole). However, when a shot of this elevator is shown, it has the same hole that the other elevator has (better seen in slow motion).

Sweeney Todd (2007)

Based on the location of the barber's chair with the picture window in Todd's barber shop and the layout of the exterior of the building, there is no possible way that the chute behind the chair would be able to dump the bodies directly into the basement without going through the center of Ms. Lovett's shop.

Thunderball (1965)

When the Disco Volante separates to escape the cruisers firing on it, the "cocoon" is seen facing the pursuing ships stern first. When the shot changes to show the gunners firing on the ships the back half of the "cocoon" has turned completely around; the gunners are firing from the separated mid section of the Volante and the stern of the "cocoon" is now facing away from the cruisers, making it easy to see which parts of the scene were filmed live and which were done in the studio.

Toy Story (1995)

When Rex shakes the table causing the baby monitor to fall, the batteries fall out and we see the open battery compartment with markings for positive (+) and negative (-), and space for two AA batteries. Woody jumps off the bed and places the two batteries inside the compartment, but before he closes the compartment note the position of the battery closest to the top of the monitor. The positive side is actually where the negative side should be so the monitor should not work, but the monitor turns on just in time to hear the soldier's warning. (00:13:15)

Buena Vista

Vacation (2015)

When Rusty is talking to the trucker on the C.B. radio, he hands the microphone to Kevin. Kevin never presses the talk button on the microphone when he is talking to the trucker.

THE END

Thank you for buying this book! I hope you enjoyed it, and if so please tell your friends, share it, lend it...spread the word! I'd love to hear any suggestions, corrections, thoughts and opinions - please get in touch at jon@moviemistakes.com. And please leave a review on Amazon - if you like this, there's plenty more where this came from. And if you've got any observations of your own, please submit them to moviemistakes.com and let other people know about them!

Made in the USA
Monee, IL
28 December 2019

19616368R00122